And Peakie Lived
Happily Ever After

And Peakie Lived Happily Ever After

Lavinia Russ

THE BODLEY HEAD
LONDON SYDNEY TORONTO

The author and the publisher wish to thank the following for permission to reprint the selections listed below: HOUGHTON MIFFLIN COMPANY for five lines from Amy Lowell's poem, "Patterns," which appear on pages 28 and 29.
GEORGE SASSOON for Siegfried Sassoon's poem, "Everyone Sang," which appears as the epigraph.

SBN 370 00973 8

Printed in Great Britain for
The Bodley Head Ltd
9 Bow Street, London WC2
by Unwin Brothers Limited
Woking and London
First published by Harcourt, Brace & World, Inc.,
New York, 1968
First published in Great Britain 1969

For—
Eva Mills and Liza Russ

Everyone Sang

Everyone suddenly burst out singing;
And I was filled with such delight
As prisoned birds must find in freedom
Winging wildly across the white
Orchards and dark green fields; on; on; and out of sight.

Everyone's voice was suddenly lifted,
And beauty came like the setting sun.
My heart was shaken with tears; and horror
Drifted away. . . . O, but everyone
Was a bird; and the song was wordless; the singing will
never be done.

—Siegfried Sassoon

One

NOBODY ever tells you how they felt when they were growing up. Not how they really felt. Maybe they can't remember. But I *know* how I feel. I am the loneliest person in the world. There is no one in the whole round world that is all by herself the way I am all by myself. I'm almost twelve, and I have a square face. Beatrice walked right into my room one night. She didn't knock. Nobody ever knocks on doors in my family the way they do in books. I had lighted the candles on the table that's in front of the mirror, and I had a long piece of rose-coloured stuff I'd found in the attic wrapped around me like a dress. Beatrice said, "What on earth are you up to now?" I was getting dressed up to give a dinner party for some English people I had just met in *The Scarlet Pimpernel,* but I wasn't going to tell her that, so I didn't say anything. Beatrice gave one of her new grown-up shrugs. "Well, I wouldn't waste any time looking at yourself. I can tell you, you look absolutely absurd." She slammed the door as she went out.

Beatrice is my sister. She's seventeen because she's al-

ways as old as the year is, or the last part of it. And this year is 1917. She has curly hair and three Best Friends, and I can't stand her. She took me out in the field next to our place last winter and said, "Lie down." There was snow on the ground, and the frozen weeds stuck up in my back. Beatrice sat on my stomach. She said, "Stop that snivelling, Peakie. Now you listen to me. You must stop trying to talk to Mother. There is a great chasm between Mother and you, and you mustn't try to bridge it." She made me repeat, "There is a great chasm between Mother and me, and I mustn't try to bridge it," three times before she would let me get up. I ran straight to the house to look for Mother. She was sitting in the back room, listening to Caruso on the Victrola.

"Mother," I said, "'Beatrice just made me—"

Mother held up her hand. "Hush. Don't interrupt Caruso." When he'd finished, she turned off the Victrola, and I told her. She burst out laughing. "Beatrice had probably just read that expression, and she wanted to try it out."

"But what does it mean?"

"Go and look it up in the dictionary. Only look up chasm, not shasm. Shasm!" Mother said, and started to laugh again.

That's the trouble with Mother. You never know when she's going to laugh. I said, "Mother, don't get mad at me, but I don't think mothers ought to laugh at their children." She didn't get mad. And that's another thing—you never know when she's going to get mad.

She said, "I'm not in the least mad. But don't tell me about what mothers ought to do. Write it down in a book. Write down everything you think I do or your father does that's wrong. Then, when you're grown up and have children of your own, you'll remember." She went to a drawer in the highboy, took out a notebook, gave it to me, and said, "You can start right now." I put "Don't laugh at your children" on the first page.

There are quite a few pages filled now with things mothers shouldn't do. There's nothing about what fathers shouldn't do because Father never does anything wrong. He is my friend. He's been my friend ever since I was eight years old in Colorado. We go out there a lot because it's so hot at home here in Missouri. "Nobody was supposed to live in Missouri but gophers and Indians," Mother says. I was eight years old, and I was watching him fish. It started to rain, and we found a cave to hide in, and he took a book out of his pocket. It was *Peter Pan,* which we'd been reading, and when he came to the part where Tinker Bell is dying and Peter says if you believe in fairies you can save her, Father shouted, "I believe!" I shouted "I believe!" too, and he has been my friend ever since.

One thing I put in the Book in big letters is "Mothers Should Send All Their Daughters to School." Beatrice goes to school. She gets to ride into Kansas City every morning with Father in one of our Fords. We have two because Mother calls up the Ford place every spring and says, "This is Mrs. John Maston. I want my usual order of a sixth of a dozen Fords." Father leaves Beatrice at Miss Barstow's on his way to the Store. That's where Father works, where he is president. It isn't really a store—it's a square stone building on Broadway with thousands and thousands of pills and bottles of medicine in it that they sell to people who have drugstores, but everybody calls it the Store. And I'm left at Marlborough with Mother and Benny and Manuel.

I go to a pretend school. There are two school desks with school chairs connected to the desks on the porch. Mother gets lessons in the mail from some place called the Calvert School, and she gives them to me. Beatrice used to sit in the front seat until she escaped to Miss Barstow's. I sit there now until Benny opens the door and says, "Lunch is on the table, Babe." And then I'm through with school. I read all the rest of the time until Father comes home with Beatrice. Mother says it's unhealthy to read all the time. She sits in the back room and reads all the time—and listens to Caruso on the Victrola. If she comes into the front room and catches me reading, she says, "Go on out in the fresh air! Do Something!" I put the book I'm reading inside my middy bloomers and read outdoors.

We didn't used to live in the country, Beatrice told me. We lived in a house on a street with a house on either side of our house. Mother said we moved to Marlborough because Father had read a book by Henry Thoreau. When I asked Father what she meant, he laughed. "Your mother was being funny. Henry Thoreau was a man who liked the country and wrote about it. I thought your mother and you and Beatrice would like the country, too."

But Marlborough isn't the country. At least it doesn't look like the way it sounds in books. And it doesn't look like any of the pictures Mother has pasted all over the wallpaper in my room— "so you will get used to living with masterpieces"—green, with lavender hills and lacy trees and valleys with streams and pretty cottages or castles in them. There's a lot of space in front of our house that's supposed to be green, but it turns brown before it's been green for more than a minute and it stays that way until it gets covered with snow. Father has planted trees all around that he says will be beautiful someday, but they're like thin little branches from a big tree now.

There's a street in front of the house and a sidewalk with cracks in it, but there aren't any other houses on it except the Kingsleys' house that's on the way to the streetcar and the Ryans'—they have a square red brick house that's the other way—past a kind of field.

I went down there once. I couldn't count the children, there were so many playing in the kitchen and out in the back field that had piles of cans and boxes in it. Mr. Ryan told me he was a conductor on the Santa Fe. "There is a town named after me," Mr. Ryan said. "In Kansas. My name is right there on the sign on the roof of the station. Ryantown, it says."

When I told Mother, she said, "Very interesting, but I don't want you to go down there again. He may have a town named after him, but he also has a big, dirty Irish family—a shanty-Irish family. Stay away from them. You might catch something."

I told her, "They are not dirty. Just kind of messy." I didn't tell her there was a funny smell in the house—it smelled like a washrag you had used too long. "There's a girl down there who is exactly as old as I am, and she took me up to their third floor and there's nothing in it now, but she says when she gets to be eighteen, her father's going to fix it up like a ballroom and give a big ball for her."

Mother said, "That's a very sad story. And she'll be

lucky if she lives to be eighteen in all that shanty-Irish mess, but I still say, don't go down there."

I don't see how Mother can talk against Irish people. She's Irish. Half Irish, anyway. Gammie was Irish, and she was teaching school in her bare feet back in Ohio when Gampie married her. That was before they came out here so Gampie could make saddles for the cowboys. He may have made that up about the bare feet—he makes fun of people as much as Mother does—but I'll bet his story about Gammie running down to the saddlery store, crying and saying, "Wid, Wid, there are Indians in the back yard!"—and Gampie shouting at her, "Well, go back and give them something to eat!"—is true, because Gammie is little and scared-looking and Gampie is tall with a big white moustache and he shouts all the time when he's talking.

That whole family makes fun of people. Uncle Ned told Mother, right in front of me, "Hadley, you ought to get Peakie a bulldog. With that square haircut and that middy blouse and bloomers, she'd look just like Buster Brown." He's a terrible man. He always has a big piece of tobacco in his mouth, and he spits out brown goo, and he hasn't got a thumb on one hand. Father says to be nice to him because a streetcar ran over his hand. He had had so much to drink that he went to sleep on the streetcar tracks and the streetcar ran over him, but then he married the cook who worked next door to Gampie's house and he doesn't drink any more.

They all make fun of people except Uncle Henry, and he's dead. He was sick for a long time in the big front room upstairs in Gampie's house. He used to sit in the sunshine by the big window, and he would take me on his lap and tell me stories. I don't remember the stories, but I remember he always said at the end, "And they lived happily ever after." Mother says I can't possibly remember that—that I was too young—but she's wrong. She doesn't remember what you can remember. Remembering is the way it is on the train to Colorado when you go through all those tunnels, one right after the other. It's black with nothing in it, and then suddenly you are out in the sunshine and everything you see out of the window is clear, like a picture in a book, and then you're back in the tunnel again. I can remember the last time I saw Uncle Henry. It was the first time I saw Father cry. He carried me on his shoulder into the front room, and Uncle Henry was lying flat in a big bed, and he looked up at me and said, "Don't forget, Peakie, they lived happily ever after." Father walked very fast out of the door, and when he put me down in the hall, he was crying.

I cry quite a lot. I cry when I'm memorizing some of the poems in *The Oxford Book of English Verse* that I'm going to say for Father when he takes me for a walk after supper. I am going to be a poet, or I am going to save the coloured people. I guess save isn't the right word. Father told me all about Lincoln last spring. I told him, "Then I could start a place for them to live in and have fun, like the place Jane Addams has up in Chicago for poor children. Wouldn't that be a good idea?"

Father said, "I don't think it is a very helpful one. They have to live separated from white people now—that's a big part of their trouble." And he's right. When we drive Benny home, we take her to a crummy-looking house on a street with a lot of other crummy-looking houses close together and garbage cans right out on the sidewalk with messy stuff spilled around them, and there's nobody but coloured people on the street.

Benny is the only coloured person I know. I have seen her son—his name is Willy, and Benny says he can't get a job—but I don't know him like I know Benny. Manuel isn't coloured—he's a Filipino. Mother met him at the Y.M.C.A. He had run away from an Army officer at Fort Riley. The officer didn't pay him anything—he pretended there was still slavery in the United States—but he had brought Manuel all the way from the Philippines, and he was awfully mad at Mother when he found out Manuel was our cook. But she talked right back to him. Mother isn't afraid of anybody. I guess I don't really like Manuel. He giggles when there isn't anything to giggle at, and he's short. I like tall people like Father. Manuel has pictures of ladies pasted all over the wall of his room in the little house he lives in next to the garage. I'm not supposed to go down there, but I went on the porch and peeked in the window and saw the ladies. They weren't Filipino ladies.

But I love Benny. She doesn't read very much, but she lets me tell her all about what I'm reading while she's working, and she lets me practise saying the poem I'm learning for Father to her. Sometimes when I act out the poem I'm learning, she stops working to watch. She always claps at the end. She never makes fun of me. She teases me sometimes. When Mother and Father are away and I want to sleep with her for company—her room is right next to mine at the top of the stairs—she always reminds me about the first time I slept with her and was so surprised when she took off her uniform that I said, "I thought the dark part stopped under your dress." But she knows that was when I was very young. Benny is my friend. I told Father, "Benny's my friend. And you're my friend. But I wish I had a Best Friend like Beatrice has. She has three Best Friends, and I haven't even got one."

We walked along the road in the dark, and then Father said, "I think we'd better plan on getting you to school pretty soon."

"Now, right now? Oh, please, Father!"

"No, not right now. You'll have to finish up this year with the Calvert School. But next year we'll figure out something." We turned around to go back home. Suddenly Father said, "I know! Until you go to school and meet some other girls, why don't you find a friend in one of the books you read?"

Father really is a remarkable man! I told him, "Father, I've already tried that."

"No!" Father said.

"Yes, yes, I have! I sat one whole afternoon in the attic and looked out of that little window—you know, the one that faces where Kansas is?—and I thought about Dorothy, the one in all those Oz books. But I decided she was too young, and she lives on a farm and I want to live in the city."

"You really like the city so much?" Father asked.

"I like all the people in the city—I like to look at the ones that walk by Gampie's house, and I like it at night when I go to bed and see the light from the street lamp on the ceiling. And 'hear the grown-up people's feet still going past me on the street.' "

Father said, "Robert Louis Stevenson?"

"Robert Louis Stevenson," I said, and we shook hands. We always do that when one of us guesses right. "But I decided I didn't want Dorothy for a friend anyway. The Tin Woodsman and that Lion and all those wild people in Oz would be fun to meet, but I thought I'd get awfully tired of them after a while. I've thought about all the girls in those Dickens stories, too."

"Now, Peakie," Father said, "you can't tell me you've read all of Dickens."

"Oh, no, but I've read all those shortened-up stories in my *Complete Book of Facts and Fancies.*"

"A bad mistake," Father said.

"Dickens is a bad mistake?"

"No, but those shortened-up stories are."

"Well, anyway, I wouldn't even want to meet any of those Dickens girls—they're always fainting or dying or something."

"What about one of the March girls?"

"What March girls?"

Father stopped walking. "You haven't read *Little Women*?" When I said, "No," he grabbed my hand. "Come on, hurry! We have to hurry so you can get to bed in a hurry, so you can go to sleep in a hurry, so you'll be all fresh and ready to start on *Little Women* in the morning. The Calvert School can wait one day. You have to meet a family."

That's how I found Jo.

Two

I NEVER thought I'd ever say that Father was wrong, but he was. It didn't take a whole day for me to pick which of the Marches I wanted for my friend. I found out when I finished the third chapter that it was Jo. That was all I did have a chance to find out because I got sick before I could read any more. Really sick. I thought it was because I tried to be like Jo. I told Mother, "I want to stay in my room all day. I am going to be a writer."

Mother said, "Come on down when you've written the last chapter of *War and Peace*."

I took some apples like Jo did and a pitcher of water up to my room and tried to write like Jo, but after I'd eaten nine apples, I felt funny. I lay down on the bed and went to sleep. When I woke up, it was dark and I felt awful. Mother had Manuel make some orange juice. She put castor oil in it and I had to drink it, but the next day I still felt awful, and Doctor Eaton said I had scarlet fever.

I was sick for a long time in the back room downstairs, so sick I don't remember anything except the Flatiron Building. There was a photograph of it on the wall beside my bed. It's a building that comes to a point in the front, all the way up to the top. It kept getting bigger and coming at me, then it would go away for a while, and then it would come at me again. It's a building in New York. Mother is crazy about it. She's crazy about everything in New York, even if she was arrested there.

She got arrested because she scolded a policeman on Fifth Avenue. He was yelling at a boy who had brought his horse and wagon onto Fifth Avenue. The boy was a foreign boy, so he couldn't understand what the policeman was yelling, so the policeman yelled louder. Mother walked up to him and told him, "Officer, stop yelling at that poor boy."

The policeman stopped yelling at the boy. He yelled at Mother, "All right, lady! Move on, move on. Don't interfere with an officer."

Mother said, "I certainly will interfere when an officer is using his authority to be a damn bully." I guess the policeman was so surprised to hear Mother swear, because she doesn't look like a lady who would walk out into the middle of a big street to swear at a policeman—with the white ruffles she wears around her neck and down the front of her dress to hide how thin she is and her white hair that she brushes straight back into such a high pompadour she looks like that picture of the English lady on the wall in my room—that he arrested her. She called Father in Kansas City, at the Store, and told him, "John, I'm in jail. Do Something."

I found out more about Jo when I was sick, after the fever and the Flatiron Building stopped. I had a nurse who read to me and made me things to eat that we never have, custard and Jello and some sweet stuff that slides down—you don't have to chew it. Mother doesn't believe in desserts. Father says, "Your dear mother doesn't believe in anything that's good to eat since she went to Battle Creek." That's the place where Mother went when she was nervous after Uncle Henry died. Mother had stayed in at Gampie's a long time before he died—she was Uncle Henry's favourite of all the people in his family, and Gampie asked her to come in and stay with Uncle Henry until he died. Gampie always called Mother whenever there was any kind of trouble—"And he always has," Father told me. "Since she was a young girl. He thinks she's the strongest person in his family. And he's right. She is."

Battle Creek was so expensive that she had the bill framed and hung it up in the back room. Up there they don't eat white bread or hot rolls or anything but brown bread, and nothing that is sweet or fried or comes out of a can. They like a lot of light, so we don't have any curtains. A lot of air, too, so the four of us all sleep in sleeping bags on top of cots on the side porch in the winter unless we're sick. Then we get to sleep inside. They don't like dust up there either, so we don't have any rugs.

I told Mother, "When I grow up, I'm going to have white curtains with big ruffles all around them in every room and carpets that go all the way to the walls and hot rolls every single day."

Mother said, "Put it down in the Book."

Miss Olson—that was the nurse's name. I liked her very much—she had long yellow hair she wore in a braid around her head—until she left and called me up on the telephone. When I said, "Oh, I'm so glad to see you!"

she gave one of those laughs that grownups give that isn't a laugh at all and said, "You can't see me over the telephone."

Miss Olson read me the rest of *Little Women.* Or most of the rest of it. She cried when she read about the time Jo took Beth to the seashore. I started to cry, too, when Beth says, "Jo, dear, I'm glad you know it. I've tried to tell you, but I couldn't." Jo knew Beth was going to die without anybody's having to tell her. That's what happens when people love other people. They know about each other without having to tell each other. I'm sure that's the way it is. If they're people like Jo and Beth.

I told Miss Olson, "I try to think about the way I would act if I was going to die."

Miss Olson frowned. "Little girls shouldn't think about dying."

"Why not? I think it's very interesting. I make up speeches before I go to sleep about what I'm going to say when I die. I know I won't be brave like Beth, though. I'll run and find Father wherever he is and get into his lap. I don't care how big I am."

I knew right away that Beth couldn't be my friend. I'd have to be very noble all the time because she was very noble. I thought about having Meg for a while—she and Jo had good times together—until Meg got married. She got very boring after that. I never even considered Amy. She's stuck-up, and she looks at herself all the time in the mirror because people tell her she's pretty. I guess she is pretty, but I'm sure she has a tiny little mouth. I have a small mouth, but I put a finger in each side and stretch it every time I'm by myself and remember, so I'll have a big mouth by the time I'm Beatrice's age. I hated Amy the first time I met her. I still hate her. It makes me furious she got Laurie instead of Jo—and it always will.

I never thought Laurie wouldn't marry Jo. I didn't know he didn't marry her until Mother took me to a play about *Little Women* to celebrate that I was over the scarlet fever. When she said, "I'm not taking you unless you've finished the book. It would spoil the ending for you," I lied to her. I told her Miss Olson and I had finished it. When Amy came back from that trip to Europe and was married to Laurie, I jumped up from my seat and yelled, "He marries Jo!"

Mother said, "Pick up your coat and tam-o'-shanter. We're leaving." She made all the people get up out of their seats so we could get out.

I asked her when we got outside, "Did we have to go because I embarrassed you—yelling like that?"

"We had to go because you told a lie. You couldn't embarrass me," Mother said.

She embarrasses other people—all the time. When she took me to my first moving picture—she loves moving pictures—it had cowboys in it, and when they went into a saloon where there were girls in short dresses with feathers in their hair and when the cowboys started to have drinks and shoot each other, Mother put her hand over my eyes and said out loud, "Don't look, Peakie," and everybody in the dark laughed.

I told Jo in my mind that I wished Mother was more like Marmee, her mother. Marmee never embarrasses her daughters. Jo thought that maybe my mother wanted to be an actress. She makes speeches all the time. I'm not sure. When she's dressed up, she's pretty enough to be an actress, with those dresses with the ruffles and the capes she has and the high fur hat she wears in the winter. "My Cossack hat," she calls it. But most of the time she goes around Marlborough in a nightgown because it's so hot, or when it's cold, she puts on one of the Japanese kimonos she sends all the way to San Francisco for. I think she could be president of something, if they had lady presidents. And she is always making speeches in a voice you can hear in the next room. It isn't loud, but you can always hear it. She has a soft voice when she talks about Caruso or reads Father something from a book by Henry James or about starving children in China from *The Kansas City Star*. The only time she used the soft voice to me was when she was sick. I came in, and she took hold of my hands and said, "Oh, her little hands are chapped." It was wintertime, and I hadn't put my mittens on. Then she looked up and laughed to Father. " 'Mimi, your little hands are cold.' "

That's another way she's different from Marmee. If she isn't making speeches, she's quoting, and she doesn't always quote things that I know. When I ask what she means, she waves her hand and says, "Oh, never mind. It's not important." But it's important to me. I don't know whether she's saying something nice about me or something terrible. I usually can ask Father and he'll tell me —like about Mimi. She was a lonely lady, he said, that died in a cold attic in an opera.

But the day Mother called me "Pavlov's dog" when she found me crying over "The Lady of Shalott"—I always cry when I get to the end and Launcelot says, "She has a lovely face; God in His mercy lend her grace, The Lady of Shalott."—Father was at the Store, so I didn't know until he came home that it was all right. Pavlov was a scientist who had a dog that always drooled at the same thing, at the same time, just the way I always cry at the same lines in "The Lady of Shalott."

Or if she isn't quoting something, she's laughing at something or doing something to make other people laugh. Like in Denver at the Brown Palace. She told Father and me to go down to the dining room first. When she walked in and sat down, she had that look she always gets when she's doing something funny. Her eyes get very big and bright blue—they're pretty blue anyway, but they get bluer. She said, "How do you like the trimming on my hat?" She was wearing her straw hat with the big brim —"My Milan Sailor." She had stuck the top of a pineapple on the crown of it. "This is where your father and I spent our honeymoon," she said—right in front of the waiter. "I thought I should wear something to celebrate."

She looked at Father. They both laughed. I didn't laugh. I wanted to go right through the floor. I will never wear the top of a pineapple on my hat. I don't have to put that down in the Book. I never will. Never.

But I don't care now. I don't care when people look at her when she's doing something funny. I don't care when she doesn't use her soft voice to me. I don't care when Beatrice goes off with Father in one of the Fords in the morning. I don't care when she comes back with one of her three Best Friends or when they get in her treehouse and I start up the ladder and she says, "You can't come up. You're too young to understand what we're talking about," and they start to giggle. I don't care. I have Jo. I have Jo to talk to.

I never talk out loud to Jo. I did, just once, and of course Beatrice caught me. "Who are you being today, Peakie?" she asked me. "Are you Joan of Arc today? You know, she heard voices, too." Jo is just around. She hears the things I hear and she sees the things I see, and they aren't as bad or they are more fun because she's around to hear and see them, too.

Sometimes we argue. Not out loud. When I walked up to see the birds that live near the Kingsleys' house—the guinea hens that say, "Puffed Rice! Puffed Rice!"—their babies ran out on the road. They looked like round balls of cotton with little sticks for legs. When I tried to pick one up, it ran fast back to its mother. I told Jo, "I am going to have eight children when I grow up. All girls." Jo thought that was silly. She was just as silly. She wants eight boys. I wouldn't know what to do with boys.

The only boy I know is the Kingsley boy, and he shot me. He's my cousin because his mother is Mother's cousin because her father was Gampie's brother. They are the elegant side of the family, Mother says, because Gampie's brother had a bank and Gampie just made saddles—and Gampie's brother was an officer in the war, a real officer in the Civil War, on the Northern side of the war. When Gampie told me, "I was in the war, too—where the bullets were the thickest. I drove an ammunition wagon," and when I didn't laugh, he said to Mother, "What's the matter with that child, Hadley? She's got the solemnest face outside a Presbyterian Church."

Kirk, that's the Kingsley boy's name, came down to Marlborough when he was home from the school he goes to in the East somewhere. I was sitting on the big bed in the back room. When he asked me, "What are those two funny little houses for out in your yard?" I told him, "That's where we sleep in the summertime. Beatrice and I sleep in one, and Mother and Father sleep in the other. I have to go out first of anybody, but I don't go to sleep until I see Father come out with Mother."

"You can't see him in the dark," Kirk said.

He's good-looking, almost as good-looking as Laurie, but he hasn't got black curly hair like Laurie. And he isn't polite like Laurie. I told him, "I can too see him in the dark. I can see his white nightshirt. I can even see his watch and his wallet and his pistol."

Kirk said, "Don't be silly. He hasn't got a pistol."

I said, "He has too got a pistol. It's right in that top drawer in the highboy."

Kirk opened the drawer, took out Father's pistol, pointed it at me, and shot me.

He didn't hit me. He hit the mattress right under where I was sitting. Benny and Manuel came running into the room, and pretty soon Father came in—somebody must have called him. Mother wasn't there—she was away somewhere. Everybody hugged me and told me how brave I was. I had just sat there. I hadn't cried or anything.

I wasn't really brave. It happened so fast that I didn't have time to get scared. I didn't tell anybody that. I just sat there and let them hug me and tell me how brave I was. Jo knew. And Jo knew why I didn't tell them. That's why she is a really, truly Best Friend.

Three

MARLBOROUGH isn't such an awful place since I found Jo. Even the afternoons aren't so awful. And they are the most awful time of the whole day when you are by yourself—even birds know that: they sound happy in the morning, but if you listen to them in the afternoon, they sound sad. Now, when I'm being somebody else or going some place else, I have Jo to watch me.

In the flower garden she watches when I am an English lady and I walk down the patterned garden paths in my stiff brocaded gown with my powdered hair and my jewelled fan and all the daffodils are blowing and the bright blue squills. There aren't any daffodils in our garden, mostly zinnias, with their bottom leaves brown because it's so hot, and I don't know what blue squills look like. But if you're acting, you have to act as if things were there that aren't there. I walk down to the wood bench that Manuel made, and I read the letter that was brought to me this morning by a rider from the Duke:

"Madam, we regret to inform you that Lord Hartwell
Died in action Thursday se'nnight."

In the poem he was:

> "Fighting with the Duke in Flanders,
> In a pattern called a war."

Jo doesn't like it when I shout the last line of the poem, "Christ! What are patterns for?" because her father was a kind of minister, so he was against using the Lord's name in vain, but when some people get all wrought up, it helps them to swear. So the Lord knows it really isn't in vain, Father says, and it's all right.

On rainy days in my room Jo looks out of the attic window in London with me, at the chimney pots on the roofs, while we wait for the Indian gentleman to climb over the roofs to find his monkey and the little princess. I'm always the little princess.

Sometimes I have Jo play Lady Patsy when we turn my dolls' house into the Racketty-Packetty House. I have to tell her what to do. She's not a very good actress. She dashes around and tears her hair, and wrings her hands and points accusing fingers, like people in the moving pictures, which is very old-fashioned, Mother says.

My dolls' house isn't really a dolls' house. It's a tall thin brown house with curlicues around the roof like a Swiss chalet, Father says, that he had built for doves, but the doves flew away. It's next to the weeping willow tree that was there before we came, so it's big enough for me to climb up to the lowest branch and practise the poem for Father while I wait for him to come out from supper and talking with Mother. "Bright star, would I were steadfast as thou art—Not in lone splendour hung aloft the night," sounds much better up there at night than it does down on the ground. The dolls' house isn't really a dolls' house, though my old dolls' furniture is down there, and I'm too old to play with dolls anyway, and too old to read *The Racketty-Packetty House,* too, but I hate to give up the family that live in it, especially Peter Piper—They have such a laughing time together, even though they are so poor.

It's funny, in books. Poor families have so much more fun than rich families—*The Racketty-Packetty House* family, and the *Five Little Peppers* family, and the *Mrs. Wiggs of the Cabbage Patch*'s family. And of course, the *Little Women*'s family. Pollyanna's and Heidi's families are poor, too, but Pollyanna is so good, she's disgusting. Heidi is all right when she's up in the mountains, but she gets awfully good when she goes to the city and meets that girl who is an invalid. There were an awful lot of invalids back in the old days. And I'm sure Lord Fauntleroy had more fun when he was poor and he and Dearest lived in New York before they went to England and he got to be a lord and rich.

I wanted to be poor, too, until we went to see Molly after she got married, and I went inside Benny's house to take her some medicine. Molly is a friend of Mother's. She is a waitress Mother met when Leah Baumann came to Kansas City to start a labour union and stayed at Marlborough. Mother and Father and I had gone to Molly's wedding. We didn't go to a church because her priest was mad at her for getting mixed up in the unions. We went downtown to the City Hall and walked down a long corridor to a room like Father's office at the Store, only bigger and with taller windows that needed to be washed. Molly was waiting for us, Molly and a man in a navy suit with water, or something, on his hair that made him look as if he'd just gotten out of the bathtub. Molly was the first bride I'd ever seen, but she didn't look like the pictures I'd seen of brides: she didn't have on a white dress or a white veil. She didn't have a bouquet. She had on a navy suit, too—it was the same suit she had on when I went to a meeting at the Labour Temple with Mother.

Mother ran up to her and kissed her. "We must be early—we're the first ones here."

"No," Molly said. "There isn't anybody else coming. Our families won't come to see us get married."

"Well," said Mother, "aren't we a lucky family to be invited!" She turned to Father. "John, I don't think you've met Gavin. He's the lucky man—no, I'm not going to say that. They are both lucky to have each other."

Father smiled and said, "I'm sorry, I forgot something. Can you wait a few minutes?" When Molly nodded, he walked out of the door very fast. When he came back, he had an armful of pink roses, all loose with their long stems sticking out every which way. He handed them to Molly. She didn't say a word. She smiled at Father; she smiled at Gavin; she took hold of Gavin's arm. They turned and walked through a wooden gate into the next office.

Mother leaned up and kissed Father. "John," she said, "let's get married."

It was the first time, I told Jo on the way home, I ever

felt exactly the same way Mother felt: I wanted to get married, too. I felt that way until Father and I took the wedding present to Molly. When we got back to Marlborough, Leah Baumann was there.

"Did you see Molly?" she asked.

"Yes," I said, and started to walk up the stairs.

"What's the matter? Is Molly sick?"

"No, but—"

"No, but what, Peakie?"

"Oh, Leah, they live in such an awful place!"

"What's the matter with it?"

"There's an awful smell in the hall before you get up to where they live—it's a kind of cabbagy smell. And then when you do get up there, it's not a house at all, it's one room. Just one room!"

Leah looked up at me—she's a grown lady, but she's miles shorter than I am. "You've just been exposed to two of the great advantages of poverty: bad smells and no privacy. But Molly and her husband are lucky. At least they have one room all to themselves."

"That's lucky? One room for two grown-up people?"

Leah patted my hand. "When you come to New York, I'll take you down to the East Side where I grew up. You'll see why I say they're lucky."

I guess she would have called Benny lucky, too, if she had seen her room, because she had it all to herself. But it wasn't much bigger than the closet in my room, because she couldn't afford a bigger one even though Mother pays her more than the other maids in Kansas City. She has to give most of her money to Willy until he finds a job. I found out Mother paid her more than the other maids when Aunt Cornelia came out to Marlborough.

She's not really my aunt. She's a friend of Mother's—they went to parties together when they were young, and I was named after her, named after her last name, which is why I have such a crummy name like Peake, instead of a pretty name like Guinevere or Annabelle Lee.

"Hadley, dear," she told Mother—after they'd said hello and how's John and how's your father and where do you want to sit—"I came out to ask you to come to the Circle. We meet every Wednesday, you know, at St. Andrew's. We make clothes and mend clothes for the deserving poor. We do need your help, dear."

"I don't sew," Mother said.

"Perhaps Beatrice would sew for us at home," Aunt Cornelia said, then looked at me and smiled. She's a very pretty lady. She's the only lady I've ever seen who wears a black velvet band around her neck, besides Napoleon's wife. "Maybe even Peake might—"

"Neither one of them can sew," Mother said.

"Why, Hadley, that's shocking! They should start to learn at once. It will help develop their characters."

Mother said, "If they have to sew to develop their characters, their characters haven't a Chinaman's chance. Let them learn how to develop their brains. Then they can hire somebody to sew for them." Mother stopped to pull in a big gulp of air—she always does that just before she says something awful. "They can hire some of your poor, Cornelia. Your deserving poor."

"Now, Hadley," Aunt Cornelia began.

"Now Hadley nothing!" Mother said. "Now Cornelia is more like it. You and your St. Andrew's Circle don't pay your maids enough to live like decent human beings, let alone buy decent clothes. They have to wear your hand-me-downs, and they have to act grateful for them, God help them. You stick them up in rooms in your attic where they freeze in the winter and boil in the summer. You expect them to be at your beck and call from morning until night. Then you quiet any pangs of conscience you might have by sewing—sewing once a week. For the poor. For the deserving poor. You make me sick, Cornelia, really sick."

Aunt Cornelia's neck got pink. "Hadley, it's about time you learned you can't go against things as they are."

"Why can't I?"

"Because you have to be realistic and accept things the way they are."

"I've noticed that whenever people say you have to be realistic, what they're really saying is: you have to think the way they think. If Columbus or Magellan, or whoever it was, had been realistic and accepted things the way they are, they'd have gone on thinking the world was flat, and you and I wouldn't be sitting here right now in the middle of America arguing."

"Oh, Hadley, that's different! You can't change the social pattern. When you try, you just make people discontented and cause trouble—the way you have, Hadley. Your maid has told other people's maids the ridiculous amount you give her. Now they want more, too."

Mother leaned forward in her rocker. "That's just the

beginning. I'm going to see that other working women get a decent wage, too, like those poor girls at Fred Harvey's lunch counter—"

"Why, Hadley Maston! Fred will never speak to you again if you—"

Mother interrupted her. "I'll have to struggle along without Fred Harvey's saying how do you do to me on Petticoat Lane. Because I'm going to do it."

"How, Hadley?"

"I'm going to help them form a union."

"Hadley! A union?"

"That's right. A union."

Aunt Cornelia shook her head. "That is the most shocking thing. I—I can't believe it. It was shocking enough when you made poor dear John move out here away from all his friends—and your friends, Hadley—way out here where nobody ever sees you any more. But unions! I feel sorry for poor dear John. That's all I can say."

"That's enough." Mother stood up. "I can take care of poor dear John without any help from you, Cornelia Peake, thank you just the same."

Aunt Cornelia stood up. "I think I had better go now," she said. She opened the screen door and started down the porch stairs.

"Come back when you want me to sew for the Undeserving Poor," Mother called to her. She turned to me. "Go get my kiki bowl," she said. Her kiki bowl is a brass bowl with water in it, where she puts her cigarettes when she's finished with them. She calls it her kiki bowl because she calls anything that's messy "kiki," and that bowl is certainly messy, but she's afraid of fires so she puts out her cigarettes in it.

After she had her kiki bowl on the table by her rocking chair and had lighted her cigarette, I asked her, "Why didn't you tell Aunt Cornelia it wasn't your idea to move out here? That it was Father's idea?"

Mother rocked back and forth and took quick puffs of her cigarette. "Because that's not the first time Cornelia Peake has called your father poor dear John. But it will be the last. She's danced with him, but she doesn't know him. She's an old maid. The only man she's ever known is her father, and he's a pompous old bully. But she thinks he's a strong man because he gives orders and pounds on the table. She thinks your father is weak because he's gentle. She doesn't know your father."

Mother stopped rocking. "Cornelia's a poor dear thing," she said. "But I was in no mood to hear her criticize your father. I can say anything I want to about my own family, but if anybody else says anything against them, I'll hit them over the head with my shillelagh." She started rocking and puffing again.

She said that because she is Irish, I explained to Jo. After Father explained it to me. Marmee, Jo's mother, never talks like that. She probably never even heard of a shillelagh.

Four

I THINK I would have run away from home if I hadn't had Jo the night Beatrice was getting dressed for a party. It was going to be a real party, with boys there, and Mother was running around as if Beatrice was Queen of the Nile. I was so disgusted, I shut my door so I wouldn't have to hear her and Benny oohing and aahing, but Mother yelled, "Peakie, come on in here and look at your sister."

I went into Beatrice's room. There she was, standing in the middle of the room, in a white dress with a pattern of little flowers all over it and a wreath of the same kind of flowers—only real—on her head.

Mother said, "Doesn't your sister look beautiful? Perfectly beautiful?"

Beatrice said, "Oh, please, Mother!"

I looked at her. I couldn't believe it. She was crying. She never cries. "What are you crying about?" I asked her.

"Oh, mind your own business," Beatrice sniffled.

Mother looked up at her; she was sitting on the floor doing something to the bottom of Beatrice's dress. "You *are* crying! What in God's name have you got to cry about? You'll be the loveliest-looking girl at the party. You can bet your boots there won't be another girl there with a dress designed by Botticelli. You're the spitting image of his 'Primavera.' "

"I don't want to look like the spitting image of his 'Primavera.' I want to look like Peggy. Her mother got her dress at Emery Bird's."

"Fiddle," said Mother. "You don't want to look like anybody else. You certainly don't want to look like a meat-packer's daughter. Just go over and look at yourself in the mirror. You look exactly like the 'Primavera.' Go on. Look at yourself."

Beatrice walked over to the mirror. She did look like the lady with the flowers in that picture that's on my wall. I could tell she thought so too, because she stopped sniffling, and she straightened the wreath on her head. I walked out of the room.

"Poor Peakie," I heard Mother say. "She's jealous. Well, she's going to have to learn to be smart because she's never going to be pretty. Put your carriage boots on, Beatrice. Your father's waiting in the car for you."

The first thing I thought when I heard that was, I'll run away. But then I thought, where would I run to? If I went to Gampie's, he'd just call up Father, and Father'd come for me. In stories, when people run away, they are always boys, and they run away to be cabinboys on ships. If girls in books are miserable, they usually have an uncle who is rich and kind who comes and scoops them up, because they look so pale and fragile, and takes them to his big house on a London square or one in a big park in the country, and he tells his housekeeper to feed them good things so they will have roses in their cheeks. Sometimes, if the girls start out as orphans, they end up as lost heiresses to emeralds and castles. But I knew Uncle Ned or Uncle Tom would never scoop me up. They aren't rich, and I'm not pale and fragile. I'm very healthy. Mother told Benny once, "Peakie is as healthy as a horse."

"She is a horse," Beatrice had said. "Ladies perspire. Horses sweat. Babe sweats all the time. Especially when she gets excited. So—she's a horse."

And, of course, I'm not a lost heiress. I know that. Father is a president, but his family never had any emeralds or castles. They had a ship once, and one of his grandfathers sailed it to China and brought back dishes like the willow plates we have with the lovers on them going over that bridge before they die, and vases like the one at Gampie's house that's on a table under the picture of "The Blue Boy" that has monkeys climbing all over it and where Gampie hides the molasses kisses.

And the other grandfather had a farm in Pennsylvania. He was a Quaker and a gentleman farmer. When I asked Mother what a gentleman farmer was, she said, "A gentleman farmer gets somebody else to feed the pigs."

I couldn't run away all by myself because I'm not smart enough. I wouldn't know what to do by myself. That's the most awful part of it all. I am not smart. I don't know how I'm going to learn to be smart. I don't even know how to look up a word in the dictionary, because if you don't know how to spell a word, how can you look it up?

I read a lot, but that doesn't make you smart. If you read a lot and don't know a lot of people to talk to, you mispronounce the words when you try to use them, or they sound different from what they mean. I thought a privet hedge was a private hedge, and a widow's mite was a widow's might—that she was a lady with a lot of muscles—until I tried to use them out loud and Mother laughed at me. I still think your peers doesn't sound like your equals, which is what it means. It sounds like people sitting up above you, like lords, and I always will think so.

And I don't understand anything about money. Anything at all. When I asked Father if we were rich or poor, he said, "We're neither. We're in between. We lean a little towards the poor side." But that didn't help.

I never have any money, real money, of my own. Neither does Mother most of the time. "I'm like royalty," she says. "I never carry money." When we go to the station (and we go there all the time because Mother says Fred Harvey has the best restaurant and the best bookstore in Kansas City), she never pays for anything. She just says, "Charge it, please."

And everybody says, "Yes, Mrs. Maston," because everybody there knows her. If she does have to give money somewhere, like at a flower store, she never waits for the change. "I'm too rich to wait for pennies," she says.

I don't think she understands any more about money than I do. Lots of times when I get to the arithmetic page in the Calvert School lesson, Mother tells me to wait a minute, she has to go in the house. Then she telephones Father at the Store. I know she does because one morning I got up from my desk and went around to the side of the porch and listened to her.

"John," I heard her say, "how do you carpet a floor that is 22 feet long and 12 feet across when the carpet is 3 feet wide? Oh, and wait a minute. How much will it cost? The carpet is $2.50 a yard." Father must have said something because Mother said, "Well, then, if you don't know, ask Miss Baker." Miss Baker is Father's secretary. "Yes, I'll wait." I ran back to my desk. When Mother came out on the porch, she had the answer.

I think it's funny the way parents think their children fall off the edge of the world the minute they leave the room. Well, it's not really funny—it's silly, but I'll never tell Mother it's silly or she might start being careful to see if I'm anywhere around before she says anything and then I'd miss learning things I learn now. And I wouldn't tell Father because it would make him unhappy. He always looks unhappy when I say anything against Mother. He thinks she's wonderful. And funny. And beautiful.

I guess she was when they got married. Aunt Hattie—she's Father's sister and she's all right except she says k-nitting instead of knitting and you're supposed to laugh, and she keeps talking about her mother's mahogany tip-top table that her cousin has and Aunt Hattie thinks she should have. That's one thing Beatrice and I agree about; if Father and Mother ever die, we're not going to fight about any mahogany tip-top table. Aunt Hattie told me that Mother and Father were the handsomest couple in Kansas City when they were young. When they danced together at parties or when they played tennis, everybody used to watch them. They play tennis sometimes now on the court here at Marlborough, but they volley all the time, and Beatrice says that's very old-fashioned. Aunt Hattie says she remembers the day Father came home and told her about Mother. He had been out hunting rabbits with Mother's brother.

Father had told Aunt Hattie, "I promised Tom I'd walk home with him. We were walking along. Tom was telling me how bored he was with the leather business—with learning about the different grades and things. We started to walk by a big red house on a corner when Tom suddenly stopped and laughed. 'Golly, this is my house.' I looked, and there, sitting on the porch, was the loveliest girl I ever saw in my life.

"Tom said, 'That's my sister there on the porch.' I wanted to say to him, 'That's the girl I'm going to marry,' but I just said good-bye instead."

Then Aunt Hattie always says—she must have told me the story a million times—"And he did marry her." Of course he married her. I know that. I know the next thing she says will be, "If your dear father hadn't been the kind boy that he was and walked home with your Uncle Tom to keep him company, you wouldn't be here." Which I think is very insulting. If Father hadn't married Mother, he would have married somebody, and I would have been his daughter, anyway. I think. I don't really *want* to think about that.

Aunt Hattie talks all the time about things that happened a long time ago. Father says it's because the past was a happier time for her than now. Aunt Hattie's husband is dead, and she hasn't any children to keep her company. "Never marry a man just because he is handsome and can sing, 'Sail, baby, sail out upon the sea, only don't forget to sail back again to me,' " Mother said.

"Hadley, dear, that's not a kind thing to say. George was a good man."

"He was good and dull," Mother said. "Hattie married him to get away from home. That's something else to remember, Peakie. Don't ever get married just to get away from home."

I didn't say it out loud, but I told Jo I'm going to get away from home a long time before I'm old enough to get married. I'm going to New York. I know I'll like it there. I can tell from the pictures in the magazines that are stacked in the attic that I look at on rainy days. All of the pictures in them are of New York or of places in the East or in England. I'll go there—to England—after I've gone to New York. The only pictures of the West have cowboys or miners in them—rough-looking men who need a shave. In the rest of the pictures the ladies and men look very elegant and rich, like the Charles Dana Gibson pictures, or they look very poor—in rags, with wind blowing the snow all over them. I've never found any pictures of poor people in the summertime—and there don't seem to be any pictures of in-between people like us.

But when I get to New York, I won't be an in-between person. I'll be rich and elegant, like a Gibson lady. If I can learn to be smart about money. If I can't, I'll live in a boarding house the way Jo did and write dreadful stories like she did and sell them to the magazines.

Jo doesn't like it when I think about running away. She's not exactly preachy about it, but she does use words

Mother calls New England words when Father uses them —like Duty and Responsibility. I don't blame her for not understanding. With a mother like Marmee, of course she would never want to run away. It's the one thing we don't agree about. No, there is another thing we don't agree about, but I never bring it up. It's done—she can't change it. But I will never understand how she could have married that old Professor Baer. I asked Beatrice once why she thought Jo married him. That was a mistake. It just gave Beatrice another chance to act grown-up.

"It's perfectly obvious. She was lonely."

"Lonely! How could she be lonely, with Marmee and Meg and Meg's family and—"

Beatrice interrupted me with her "Oh, you poor child" laugh. "You wouldn't know, of course, at your age, but there are things in life besides mothers and sisters."

"If you mean lovers and mistresses, I know all about them." It was lucky I had found out about them just the night before. I had learned a poem of Robert Herrick's to say to Father. He was a poet who lived in England way back in the seventeenth century, and Father had picked him out of *The Oxford Book of English Verse* as the next poet he would like to hear because he said he used words that sounded like what they meant.

Father read out loud, " 'Whenas in silks my Julia goes, Then, then, methinks, how sweetly flows That liquefaction of her clothes.'

"Liquefaction!" Father said. "Isn't that a fine word? Liquefaction—it sounds like her dress, doesn't it? It's a long dress and it rustles. What colour do you think it is?"

"I think it's green," I said. "Dark green, with silver in it."

"I think you're right," Father said. "That's what onomatopoetic means. It means the word sounds like what it is. Liquefaction—" He laughed. "What would Miss Baker think if I went around the Store saying, 'Liquefaction, liquefaction'?"

So I picked a poem by Herrick that was called "To My Mistress." After I said it to him, Father asked, "Do you know what a mistress is?"

"Yes. It's a lady with a big skirt and a kind of long cane with a ribbon tied on it who tends sheep."

Father said, "Not always. It can mean a lady who is a friend of a man she isn't married to."

"Why doesn't he marry her if he likes her?"

"Well, he may have a wife already."

"Then why does he need another lady to like?"

Father stopped walking. "That is a question I'm not prepared to answer. Maybe you and your mother better have a talk."

"Oh, Father! I know all about that." And I did. Mother had told me that day I ran into the house and said, "Mother, come on out! A terrible-looking dog is jumping all over Binkie!"

Mother had said they were probably trying to make puppies. Then she sat up very straight and got her funny voice and talked about people loving each other and how that made babies, and she really didn't make much sense. I asked Beatrice when she came out to bed that night. That was one time she was nice. She didn't tease me. She explained the whole thing to me. Except she forgot mistresses. And Binkie didn't have any puppies.

Binkie is an Airedale. Our other dog is named Dutch, after the Duchess of Marlborough, and she is a Great Dane. She's supposed to be our watchdog, but Binkie is the one that barks. Dutch lies under the bridal wreath bushes by the front steps and pants.

I was trying to make her stand up straight and walk by my side—I was the Duchess of Marlborough and I was walking in the gardens at Blenheim Palace—but Dutch kept wagging her tail and then flopping down on the brown grass when Father came around the corner of the house with Mother. I knew the minute I saw him something had happened. Father had the "I have a surprise for you" look on his face.

"Hello, Peakie," he said. He was pretending he had nothing to tell, but he's not a good pretender. "What are you doing?"

"Just playing with Dutch," I said, and waited.

"Well," Father said, "you won't have time to play with Dutch much longer." Then his face got crinkled up and he said, "You'll be going to school."

I burst into tears.

Mother said, "That's a fine how-de-do. Your father and I spend the afternoon getting you into a school, and all you do is cry."

Father said, "Hadley, she's happy."

Mother said, "Well, God help her husband if she bursts into tears every time she's happy."

I hardly heard her. I was hugging Father and he was hugging me, and inside I was yelling at Jo: I'm going to school!

Five

THE FIRST DAY at school was the worst day in my entire life. I don't care if perfectly terrible things happen to me when I grow up—if I'm on a ship with all my eight children and a storm comes up and washes all the sailors into the waves and I have to go down steps in the dark and find ropes and tie all my eight children to the mast and climb up to the bridge and figure out what all those instruments mean—nothing will never be as bad as the first day at school.

It wasn't a school anyway. It was a convent. A French convent. Even seeing it through Jo's eyes didn't help because she hadn't ever seen a convent either, and she was just as scared as I was.

Father took me in on his way to the Store. He stopped the Ford by a brick wall. Girls were going in through a gate, lots of girls. They all had the navy jumpers and white blouses on that I'd been measured for. And they were all little girls. They were babies! Father and I got out of the Ford and walked through a kind of court. There was a nun walking very fast through it. Father said, "Could you help us, please?"

She stopped and said something I didn't understand and Father didn't either, but she beckoned to me and Father said, "Go on with her, dear."

I started to cry.

"Peakie, Peakie," Father said, "be a brave girl. I'll be back in a couple of hours to pick you up."

He walked out of the courtyard, and I followed the nun. I followed her down a long corridor that had no rug but had straight tall chairs along each side of it that looked as if nobody ever sat in them. I followed her to a shiny wooden door. The nun knocked and said something and someone said something back to her I didn't understand, but she said it in the coldest voice I have ever heard. I was scared of who had that voice before I saw her.

There are a lot of expressions people use that don't mean anything. They are lazy expressions they use when they don't want to stop and think, Father says. He calls them "putting your elbows on the table" expressions. The minute the door opened and I saw the nun who went with that cold voice, I thought of the "elbow on the table" one Benny says all the time, "Nothing is ever as bad as it seems," and I knew it was wrong, for this nun was the scariest thing I had ever seen in my life.

She was standing with her back to a tall window. At first I could only see her outline, which was all black except for a white kind of bib and a white band around her face. She looked like something I'd seen somewhere, but I couldn't remember where. Then she spoke to the other nun, and the nun scuttled away. She said something to me as the door closed I didn't understand. A white hand came out from her black sleeve and beckoned me. "Come here," she said.

I walked up to her. "Yes, Sister," I said.

"My name is Mère Bernadette. That is the first thing you must learn."

I couldn't pronounce it, so I didn't say anything.

"Your name is Peakie?"

"Yes."

"You are to answer, 'Oui, ma Mère.' "

"Oui, ma Mère."

"Now, you have learned your first three French words." She sighed. "Some day you may learn how to pronounce them. What is your real name?"

"Peakie."

"Peakie, ma Mère."

"Peakie, ma Mère."

"That is an odd name."

"Oui, ma Mère."

"And your age is twelve?"

"Oui, ma Mère."

"Why don't you look at me, Peakie?"

I wasn't going to tell her because her voice scared me. I lifted my head and looked at her. Looked straight up into her eyes. They were blue—not the soft blue that sometimes turns to grey like Mother's, or the blue that sometimes turns to lavender like Beatrice's. They were hard blue—like a glass vase we had. They would never change to any other blue. I knew, I knew she thought I was a big, lumpy girl who had never been outside of Kansas City. I could feel my hands and feet get bigger.

"I've been to Scituate," I heard myself say. How can you say things you don't know you are going to say? I don't know but you do. Anyway, I do.

"What is that?"

"That's a place in Massachusetts. Where my father's father came from."

"Ah, your father. He is very gentle," Mère Bernadette said. Only she pronounced it gentile. "He tells me you have had a strange education, but you are a bright young girl. With a bright imagination."

Father had said that? About me? I loved him so much that minute that I said to myself, "If I ever get out of this awful place, if I ever grow up, I'll do something, something perfectly wonderful, for him. I don't know what it will be, but it will be something perfectly wonderful." Just thinking about Father gave me the courage to look at her again. And I knew where I had seen her.

"Ma Mère, I know where I have seen you before. You look like that stone saint in the tall thin picture of Chartres that's on the wall in my room."

She laughed. No, she sneered. I'd read sneer a million times, and I never could imagine what it looked like, but I knew what a sneer looked like after Mère Bernadette sneered. "You have had a strange education. Little bits and pieces, your father said. We must now fill in between the little bits and pieces. It cannot be done in one day. That is evident."

She put her thin hands up to her veil, smoothed it down, and said, "Come." She opened the door and sailed very fast down the long corridor. She didn't make any sound. I couldn't see her shoes. My brown oxfords made a terrible noise when I followed her. She suddenly turned to the right, opened a door, said something, turned to me, said, "Go in, Peakie," and sailed away.

I walked into a bare room—bare like Marlborough, without any rug or curtains. It had desks and chairs like the ones on our porch and, at the end, a blackboard. In front of the blackboard was a table, and behind the table was a nun. I looked at her. She had a moustache.

She got up and pointed to a chair. I sat down. She went out of the door. When she came back, she had a plate in her hands she put in front of me. There were two long pieces of white bread on it, with lots of butter on them. There were some chocolate squares on the plate, too.

"Thank you, ma Mère," I said.

"Ma Soeur," she said.

"Ma Soeur."

She put the chocolate between the slices of bread and put it into my hands. "Mangez," she said. "Eat," and she smiled.

I burst into tears.

She gave me a funny look as if I had frightened her, and then she put her hands up to straighten her veil just the way Mère Bernadette had, but her hands weren't long and thin like Mère Bernadette's. They were as big as mine. They were bigger—and they were red. Then she sailed out of the room.

It was the funniest sandwich I'd ever eaten, but it was the best one, too, even though it had wet spots on it because I was crying. It was the first white bread I had ever eaten. The outside was crunchy and the inside was soft.

After I finished it, I stopped crying. I had nothing to blow my nose on—so I bent down and blew it on the end of my bloomers. I sat there, and I figured out the way I would come back to see Mère Bernadette after I had become famous. I had already figured out I was going to tell Father when he came for me that I wasn't going to go to school there. I would drive up to the gate in a big, long car—with no top on it. There would be a chauffeur and a footman in the front, like the pictures by Charles Dana Gibson of the cars on Fifth Avenue that were in the magazines in the attic—the pictures, I mean. I would be sitting in the back, all alone, with a beautiful dress on, a grey-blue dress I decided, and I'd have a lot of grey-blue veils over my head and around my neck. And because I was so famous, Mère Bernadette would be standing at the gate to meet me, holding a big bunch of dark red roses, with long dark green velvet ribbons on it, to give to me.

And the footman would jump out and open the car door, and I would step down and smile at Mère Bernadette, and she would start to apologize for being so mean to me years ago, and I would tell her, in French, of course, and talking so fast she couldn't keep up with what I was saying, that so many wonderful things had happened to me since I had seen her, I didn't even remember.

I was trying to figure out what I had done that had made me so famous when the door opened and Father walked in. "Hello, Peakie dear," he said, and smiled at me. "How was your first day at school?"

"Oh, Father," I said, and burst into tears.

I have started a new section in the Book for when I grow up. It says, "What I am not going to do when I grow up." I am never going to cry. No, that's not right. I guess I'll always cry when I fall down or have a baby or things like that. Or when people die. That's all right. Grown-up people cry then. They even cry when they hear sad music or read a sad poem. But I'm not going to cry when somebody does a brave thing or when I read about somebody being brave or being proud when something terrible is happening to them, the way I do now. I've bet Jo a thousand times that I could read that part in *The Little Minister* without crying—the part about Nanny—she's a very poor and very old lady—getting ready to go to the poorhouse, but when I get to where she acts proud, even if she is old and poor and going to the poorhouse—where it says, " 'We must go,' said the doctor firmly. 'Put on your mutch, Nanny.' (That's an everyday cap old ladies wear in Scotland.) 'I dinna need to put on a mutch,' she answered, with a flush of pride. 'I have a bonnet.' "—that's where I always lose my bet and cry. If Nanny had cried, I would have felt sorry for her, but I wouldn't have cried. It's because she was proud—that's what makes me cry.

And I'm not going to cry when somebody does something kind or calls me dear, the way I do now. I cry so much now that Mother says I should have been named "Alice Ben Bolt" and then she sings, "She wept with delight when you gave her a smile, and trembled with fear at your frown."

But that's not true. I've never trembled with fear. And

Mère Bernadette could have smiled and smiled and smiled, and I wouldn't have cried. It's only when somebody like Father smiles that I cry. I can't understand why. Maybe by the time I grow up, I'll have it figured out.

Six

THE FRENCH CONVENT isn't so awful since David Hayes told me about Jane Eyre. I haven't found a Best Friend. I can't have a baby for a Best Friend. And they're all babies at the convent: the oldest one is ten, and I'm twelve, going on thirteen. But I still nave Jo, when I get home. And there's Mère Jeanne Louise—she's an English nun. She lets me call her Mother Jane when we're by ourselves for my English lesson—it's the only time in the whole day I can speak English, so it's the only time I can talk because I don't know any French yet but "oui, ma Mère" and "non, ma Mère." She is going to be my friend. She looks exactly like the picture of Queen Elizabeth, the one who was Shakespeare's friend, that's pasted on my wall. Without the ruff around her neck, of course, or the pearls sewed on her dress, but she has the same long nose, and she looks as if she could say, "Take her to the Tower!" too, any time she felt like it.

Mother Jane can laugh, too. When I told her, "I bet Falstaff's laugh was just like your laugh," (we take turns reading Shakespeare out loud) she had to pull a big white handkerchief out of her pocket and blow her nose, she laughed so hard. When she read the part about Falstaff dying—"A' made a finer end and went away an it had been any christom child. A' parted even just between twelve and one, even at the turning o' the tide. For after I saw him fumble with the sheets, and play with flowers, and smile upon his fingers' ends, I knew there was but one way. For his nose was as sharp as a pen, and a' babbled of green fields."—she had to blow her nose to keep from crying.

I have confided in her, the way you're supposed to do with a friend. "I'm not going to stay in Kansas City all my life," I told her. I was kind of afraid she might give me a lecture about being satisfied with where the Lord had put you or something, but instead she slipped her hands inside her black sleeves and nodded her head up and down.

"Oh, of course you're not," she said.

"How did you know that, Mother Jane?"

"Why, any girl with spirit wants to go looking for adventure." She laughed. "Over the hills and far away."

"Did you go looking for adventure?" I asked her.

"Of course I did. And I found it."

"Where?"

"In the order, of course."

My face must have showed what I was thinking because Mother Jane laughed again.

"You expected me to say I found it riding with a handsome sheik across the sands of Araby, didn't you? No, Peakie, I found it in the order. I found an adventure of the spirit. And that's the most exciting adventure of them all."

I believed her. I couldn't imagine it, but I believed it was true if Mother Jane said so. I know Mère Bernadette didn't join the order to find adventure: she joined it so she could become the Mother Superior and boss everybody.

"That Mother Bernadette would have been a countess in France if she hadn't decided to be a nun," Father told Mother at supper the first day I went to the convent.

"How could she have been a countess?" Mother asked. "You mean the French Revolution, the guillotine, and Sydney Carton, and 'It's a far, far better thing I have done than I have ever done before' was all a waste of time?"

"Now, Hadley," Father said. "You'll get Peakie all confused. The Mother Superior comes from an old family of aristocrats. Countess would have been a courtesy title the government would let her use."

"Well," said Mother. "I'm confused. If they're so courteous, why did they make her and the other nuns leave France?"

"Douglas Miller said—"

"Who's Douglas Miller?" I interrupted.

"He's the man that gave the nuns his mother's house," Mother said. "Go on, John."

"Well, Douglas said something about the French government confiscating church property. He's a very devout Catholic. I didn't feel like prying—"

"John," Mother said. "I wouldn't trade you for a ring-tailed monkey. But as a gossip, you are a complete failure." Father smiled across the table at her.

Beatrice said, "What's the countess look like, Babe?"

"She's very thin and tall, and she has a long, thin white

face. And the way she looks at you—she makes you feel like a—I don't know—like a—"

"Like a peasant?" Mother asked. "Does she make you feel like a peasant?"

The only peasants I've ever seen were in a picture in my room, standing in a field with their heads down, and I only know they were peasants because Father told me they were, and they were praying because a bell called the Angelus had rung. Mère Bernadette didn't make me feel the way they looked, so I didn't answer Mother, but she didn't notice.

"What I want to know," Mother said, "is—if they are all countesses—who peels the potatoes?"

"She's the only countess," Father said. "Peakie told me on the way home that the nuns who teach are called Mothers, and the ones who do the chores are called Sisters. Isn't that right, Peakie?"

"Yes, that's right."

"Obviously," Mother said, "nobody has told them about the French Revolution."

After David Hayes came, I didn't care whether Mère Bernadette made me feel like a peasant or not. I was going to be a governess, like Jane Eyre, until I was a poet or an actress.

David Hayes came out to spend the night at Marlborough. He was one of the people that Father got to come and talk in a hall downtown. Most of the people that came to talk stayed at Marlborough. That's how I saw John Cowper Powys—he was a tall man with such curly hair that it looked as if he had a hat of black feathers on his head, and he boomed out at supper, "I never pass by a beggar without giving him a coin, poor beggar!" and laughed —only he pronounced it "begga." And Dr. Grenfell, who lived up in Newfoundland and sent Beatrice and me fur-lined coats with hoods like the Eskimos wore when he got back home, and we wore them when we sat at the school desks on the porch in the wintertime, when it wasn't so cold that we had to wear our mittens. You can't write the answers with mittens on. And Leah Baumann. And Thorstein Veblen. Dr. Eaton, our doctor, came all the way out to Marlborough to scold Father about bringing Mr. Veblen to Kansas City.

"You had no business bringing a man like that to our forum, John," Dr. Eaton said. "His ideas are dangerous."

"What makes them dangerous?" Mother asked. "That they're different from your ideas? Is that what makes them dangerous?"

Dr. Eaton looked at Mother. "Hadley, I don't like to say this—"

"Then don't," Mother said.

Dr. Eaton went right on as if she hadn't said anything. "I don't like to say it, but you're in no position to talk. People are talking about your going to the Labour Temple. You're not only making trouble for yourself, Hadley, getting mixed up in something you don't know anything about, but you and your unions could hamper the preparations for war, if we get in the war. You're being very unpatriotic, Hadley, getting mixed up with unions."

"Ralph"—Mother laughed—"I always knew you were a pompous little rabbit. I never realized you were such a stupid little rabbit. Go on home, scurry back to your little warren."

"Now, Hadley," Dr. Eaton started.

"Now nothing," Mother said. "I'm surprised, now that I think about it, that you don't carry leeches in your little doctor's bag to bleed the sick, you're so out of date. Maybe you do. Oh, go on home—go home!" So we had to find a new doctor.

But David Hayes was the one who came to speak that I liked the best. He was the first Jewish man I ever met, the first half-Jewish man. His mother was all Jewish, and his father was all Quaker, like Father's cousin or aunt or something from Pennsylvania, who said "thee" instead of "you" when she talked. He had white hair, thick white hair, like Mother's, and he was thin and tall like Mother—taller—with a beautiful nose and blue eyes.

He took me for a ride in the Ford—the one for two people. The top was down, and his hair blew back in the wind and he shouted, " 'I celebrate myself!' " He turned to me. "That's Walt Whitman. Do you know Walt Whitman?"

I was afraid he'd ask me what he did, so I said, "No."

"I'm sure there is a copy of his *Leaves of Grass* around your house somewhere. Your dear father looks like a *Leaves of Grass* man to me," David said and laughed.

He stopped to read a sign at a corner. Or it would have been a corner if it had been in Kansas City. In Marlborough it was just a place where two roads met between two fields with weeds in them. "Wyandotte Street," he read on the sign. "Wyandotte Street that way. Troost Avenue that way. Which way do you want to go, my young comrade?"

"I want to go to New York," I said.

"Great!" David said. "It's a great city! And what do you plan to do when you get there?"

"I'm going to be either a poet or an actress. But I don't know how I'm going to live when I get there. I haven't any money."

"Simple," David said. "You go to a French school, your father said?"

"A French convent."

"A French convent. Perfectly simple—beautifully simple. You learn to speak French, and you can be a Missouri Jane Eyre."

"What's that?"

"Jane Eyre? She was a governess—she taught children—"

"I don't want to teach children."

"Ah, but that's just the beginning of her story. She went to teach some children—and she ended up getting everything she wanted. Though why she wanted Mr. Rochester—he was such a moody cuss—I'll never know." He turned to me. "You learn French, then you can come to New York and teach until you decide whether you want to be a poet or an actress."

"I want to have eight children, too," I said.

David laughed. "That's a lot of wanting! You may have to choose. You have to do a great deal of choosing as you grow up, Peakie. You have to choose and compare and then decide what you want the most. It's people wanting everything that makes them so unhappy. You can't be a pig." He looked at me. "You'll never be a pig, will you? Promise me, Peakie. You'll never be a pig."

"I promise I'll never be a pig."

"Good," said David. "That's settled." He started the Ford. "We'd better get back. We'll talk about your coming to New York to teach tomorrow."

But we never did. Father and I climbed up the trees and got all the chickens who roost in them and carried them down and locked them in the garage, so they wouldn't crow and wake up David in the morning. But when Benny went to tell him breakfast was ready, he wasn't there. He wrote Father in a letter that it was so still in Marlborough he couldn't sleep—he'd called a taxi and gone down to the Hotel Muehlbach. I was sorry he'd gone, but I'll see him when I go to New York. After I've learned French.

Seven

DECIDING to be Jane Eyre made the convent seem better—Jane Eyre and the Hershey Kisses. Father and Mother and Beatrice went to New York to see about Beatrice going to a college near there next year, and they left me to stay with the boarders at the convent. It was the first time I'd ever spent a night away from everybody I knew, and on top of that, I was so jealous of Beatrice—she was going to get away from Marlborough before I did, and go to New York before I did—that I couldn't eat. I had to sit there at the table and listen to the babies ask me to pass something to them in French. And listen to them giggle when I didn't know what the something was they wanted. I sat there until dinner was over and everybody folded their napkins and put them into napkin rings, except me—I didn't have a ring. Until Soeur Marie Thérèse came to the table and beckoned me to go with her. I went with her down the hall to the room where I had gone the first day and seen Mère Bernadette. She wasn't there this time. Nobody was there. Soeur Marie Thérèse pointed to a big book, the only book that was on a long table. The way she pointed I knew she wanted me to look at it, so I pulled a straight chair over to the shiny table—everything shines at the convent—and opened the book. Soeur Marie Thérèse sailed out of the room.

I'll never figure out how the nuns can sail that way when they're walking. They must have to put their feet down on the floor, but you never hear the noise that shoes make. And they never look as if they were walking. They sail, they sail along like black ships with a wind blowing them. It doesn't make any difference if they're fat or thin or tall or short—they all sail. They must learn how to do it when they learn how to be nuns.

The book had big coloured pictures of saints in it. Some of the saints had arrows or sticks stuck in them. All of them were pale. And they all looked upwards. None of them looked happy. I shut the book and walked over to the window. I could see myself in the glass: it was shiny, too. I knew I could never be a saint. I tried looking upwards, but my face wasn't thin or long like the lady saints in the book.

Maybe I could be a dancer. I've thought sometimes I might decide to be a dancer since Father took me to see Pavlova. She was a beautiful Russian lady—she came out alone on the stage up on her toes, all in white with white wings. And she kept up on her toes all the time until she fell very slowly on the ground, with her wings folded, and died. She was a swan, and a hunter had shot her.

I took off my shoes and tried to see if I could stand on my toes, and Soeur Marie Thérèse opened the door. She didn't say a word. She pointed at my shoes, beckoned me with her white hand, and sailed down the corridor. I picked up my shoes, and I followed her to a dark flight of stairs. I followed her up the stairs, down a long dark corridor, and into a narrow room with nobody in it, with nothing in it but a row of bureaus and pegs on the wall with clothes hanging on them. Soeur Marie Thérèse stopped in front of one of the pegs and pointed. My nightgown was hanging there, with Beatrice's Jaeger bathrobe. She pointed at them, pointed at me, turned, and sailed out.

I wanted to yell at her, "Say something! Say something, even if I won't understand it. Say something!" There wasn't a sound. Not any kind of sound. It was like watching a moving picture, only I was the only person watching it, and there wasn't any music to go with it.

I'm afraid, I thought, and it isn't a bit the way it sounds in books or the way Jo and I act when we pretend to be afraid, wringing our hands and fluttering around like birds. I knew the only chance I had was if I stayed still, so I undressed as fast as I could, then I stood still and waited. I had never been afraid before. Not when I was awake.

When I was little, I used to have a dream, the same dream, over and over. I'd be in the little room that was off the big upstairs sitting room at Gampie's. There would be three ladies sitting in the room, rocking. I didn't know any of them. After a while they would start throwing pots and pans at each other. They weren't mad at each other —they kept right on rocking and throwing the pots and pans. It was very noisy. When I got tired of the noise, I knew—I knew that all I had to do to wake up was to kneel down and put my head on the lap of one of the ladies—it had to be the one with the blue-and-white checked apron —and I'd smell the wet soapy smell of her apron. And I'd wake up. I was always afraid when I woke up. It scared me so that it had really worked again—waking myself up by putting my head on the blue-and-white apron—and that I knew in the dream it would wake me up, that then I'd go and get in bed with Beatrice. She'd turn over and say, "Oh, for heaven's sake," and I'd go back to sleep.

This was different. I was awake. I was all by myself. I couldn't find Jo to watch me be brave. When Soeur Marie Thérèse opened the door, it was just like the dream. I knew—I knew exactly what she was going to do. She was going to beckon to me, and I was going to follow her into a big black room. And she did beckon to me, and I did follow her into a big black room. There were white spots in the black. I knew they were cots with the babies in them. In the middle of the black there was a big bed with white curtains all around, like a square white box. I knew that was where Soeur Marie Thérèse was going to sleep. She gave me a little push and my knee hit something hard, and I knew that was the cot where I was supposed to sleep. I lay down, pulled the covers over me, and Soeur Marie Thérèse disappeared into the black.

I heard a rustling sound for a minute and then there wasn't any sound at all. I couldn't curl up in the bed. There were wires that started at the back of my neck, that went down my arms to my fingers, and down my legs to my toes. If I moved, I knew they'd go snap. I tried to think of poems I knew by heart, but I could only remember the ones with dark words in them: "O what can ail thee, knight-at-arms, Alone and palely loitering? The sedge is withered from the lake, And no birds sing." And, "I had a dove and the sweet dove died. I think it died of grieving."

I knew that very minute why Father had said it was an unkind thing to pretend to be a widow that time he came and found me kneeling by a grave in the graveyard on the other side of the streetcar tracks. I'll never pretend to be a widow or to be dying again. Death isn't funny. Mother laughed at it, and she made Aunt Tess—that's her sister—laugh at it. Up in Chicago. A long time ago.

She and Aunt Tess had had some kind of fight—Aunt Tess had said something mean about Father, so Mother wouldn't see her any more. But somehow Mother and I were in Chicago, in a hospital, and we walked into a dark room, almost as dark as the room in the convent, but I could see a lady lying in a bed. She looked like Mother, except her hair was dark, instead of white, and she looked very sad. She didn't look as if she'd just washed her face and was all ready to go on a trip the way Mother always does.

"Hello, Tess," Mother said. "Peakie and I were in Chicago and decided to come and see you."

Aunt Tess reached out her hand. "Hadley, I'm dying."

"Fiddle," Mother said, taking her hand. "Of course you're not dying. You're too ornery to die."

And Aunt Tess laughed. That was brave of Aunt Tess to laugh because she did die. I always thought it was awful of Mother to say such a mean thing to Aunt Tess when she was dying. Until that night at the convent.

Suddenly there was a soft sound in the black. I sat up straight in the bed. There was Soeur Marie Thérèse's face, close to mine. She had on a white cap like a baby's bonnet. She gently pushed me down on my pillow, she tucked the covers in around me, she put some hard things in my hand, and she was gone, back into the black. I felt the hard things. They were four Hershey Kisses. I took off the silver wrappings and ate the Kisses.

I curled up under the covers. The wires had melted—they hadn't gone snap. I made a solemn vow: I was going to learn all the French words there were, so I could talk to Soeur Marie Thérèse. So I could go to New York and be a governess like Jane Eyre. But before that, I was going to tell Mother I thought it was very brave of her to laugh about dying and to make Aunt Tess laugh. And I wouldn't care if she did say, "Oh, go on outdoors and Do Something."

Eight

I DIDN'T get a chance to tell Mother how brave she was because Jack Taylor came the day after she and Father and Beatrice got home from New York.

When I came down to breakfast, a man I had never seen before was sitting at the table. Father said, "Jack, this is Peakie. Peakie, this is Jack Taylor."

Jack said, "Hello, Peakie."

"Hello," I said, and sat down. I stared at him until Beatrice, who was all dressed up in her new green cashmere sweater, the one Mother had sent all the way to England for—all dressed up for breakfast!—she's always a mess at breakfast—she keeps Father waiting while she goes back upstairs to get straightened up—until she said, "Stop staring, Babe."

And then with her terrible imitation of a lady's laugh she said, "You'd think she'd never seen an Englishman before."

"She probably never has," Jack said. "Not a Cockney, anyway. Have you, Peakie?"

I looked straight into his eyes. They were blue. They

were the blue of the sky in the Maxfield Parrish pictures. "No," I said, and I fell right straight in love. It does happen all of a sudden, I said to Jo. Just like in the books. Jack had the blackest hair I'd ever seen, except John Cowper Powys'. But Jack's hair was short—except over the front of his forehead, where it turned into a kind of roll. His nose went straight down until it got to the very end, and then it went up. His mouth had lips—like Father's and David Hayes's and Uncle Henry's. They were the only other men I'd ever seen who had anything but a straight line for a mouth. He had on a light blue shirt and a black tie and a navy suit. He didn't have on any vest.

When Father and Beatrice and I walked out to the Ford, he walked out with us. "I'll see you again, Peakie," he said, and he put his hand up to his forehead in a salute. I looked out of the window at the back of the Ford. He was standing by the gate. He was tall and thin. And beautiful.

"He's beautiful," I said.

Beatrice—she was sitting in front with Father—turned around and made her grown-up face. She does it by lifting her eyebrows as high as she can get them. "Oh, for heaven's sake, Babe, men aren't beautiful," she said.

"Please don't call me Babe," I said. "And he is."

Beatrice shrugged her shoulders. "Jack would think it was very, very funny if he heard you say that—he'd say I.W.W.'s aren't beautiful."

"What's an I.W.W., Father?" There's really nothing you can do when Beatrice acts grown up except to pretend she isn't there.

But trust Beatrice to show off anyway. She answered, "They're men who are against governments."

"Now, Beatrice," Father said. "That's a pretty sweeping statement. They fight for the rights of working men. All over the world. That's what the I.W.W. stands for, Peakie. International Workers of the World."

I said it to myself. International Workers of the World. I counted the words on my fingers. International Workers of the World. "Where's the O.T.?"

"What are you talking about?"

"It ought to be I.W.O.T.W."

"Oh, for heaven's sake." Beatrice turned back in her seat and said to Father, "Well, if they're not against governments, why didn't Jack stand up when they played 'God Save the King'?"

"Where did they play 'God Save the King,' Father? Where did they play 'God Save the King'?"

Father said, "In New York. David Hayes took us to a play, and that's where we met Jack. In the intermission they collected money for the families of British sailors who had been torpedoed—who had been on ships that had been torpedoed, I mean."

"Like the sailors on the *Lusitania*?"

I knew the *Lusitania* was a ship that had been torpedoed because Mother had taken me to see an actress named Maude Adams, and she kept crying up on the stage, and I thought she was supposed to be crying in the play until Mother suddenly got up from her seat in the dark and said, "Come on, Peakie, we're leaving. It's a disgrace to sit here and watch that dear woman cry."

When we got out on the street, I asked Mother, "Why was she crying?"

And she told me, "Because a great friend of hers, Charles Frohman, went down on the *Lusitania* yesterday."

I knew it, too, because every time I didn't come the minute Mother called me, she always said, "Remember the two children who went down in the *Lusitania* because they didn't come up on deck the minute their parents called them."

"Not only the sailors on the *Lusitania*," Father said. "On all the ships that have been sunk."

"And Jack didn't stand up?"

"No."

"Why was he supposed to stand up?"

"Because you're supposed to stand up for your national anthem, and 'God Save the King' is his national anthem. He gave some money for the sailors—he's a sailor himself, not in the Navy, the British Navy. He sails on freighters. But he wouldn't stand up for 'God Save the King.' "

Father drove the car over the streetcar tracks. "I expect Beatrice is right. Jack is against governments."

I decided right then, if Jack was against governments, I was against governments. "Whither thou goest, I will go." That's from the Bible. That's the way women feel that love somebody, Mother said, which is pretty confusing because a girl said it to her mother-in-law in the Bible. She didn't say it to her husband—he was dead.

But a lot that Mother reads from the Bible is confusing, even though it sounds beautiful. Except the psalms

—that David wrote. Especially the one where he says, "I will lift up mine eyes unto the hills." That one's my favourite. I guess because Father read it to Mother while they were sitting under a tree in Gampie's back yard the day I was going to be born.

I didn't hear anything all day at the convent. I didn't see anybody. I was rehearsing what I was going to say to Jack when I got home. I probably won't have a chance to say anything, I told Jo. Mother will be telling him about her unions, and Beatrice will be showing off about all the books she's read. But I'm going to show him my poems. I don't care.

I was waiting at the gate when the Ford came up. There was someone in the front with Father. When I saw it was Jack, I wanted to run back into the convent. I had planned to sneak in through the kitchen when we got to Marlborough and get dressed up before I saw him again. I looked awful. My navy jumper had chalk all over it, and my white shirtwaist was mussed up, the way it always gets.

"Why is it," Mother said the first day I came home in my uniform, "that no matter what you put on, you always end up looking as if you'd just gotten off the train? And off a coach, not a pullman!"

But the minute I got in the Ford, everything was all right, the way it always is when I'm alone with Father. When I try to talk with other people, it's jerky, as if I were in a car with somebody who didn't know how to drive. No, that's not right—I feel as if I were the car. I make a lot of noise getting started, and then I lunge ahead, and I go too fast. Sometimes I stall or bump into something. But when I'm with Father, I go along smooth as can be.

It was like that with Jack there. He and Father were talking about David Hayes.

"He's a bit of a dilettante," Jack said.

"What's that mean?" I asked him, and didn't think until afterwards when I went over the conversation that I wasn't the least bit embarrassed to ask him what a word meant.

Jack turned around so he looked right at me. "In David's case, it means he dabbles in Socialism because he thinks it's romantic."

Father said, "By that definition I'm certainly a dilettante. I dabble, too. I'm curious about what new movements are doing, about what new ideas are flying around."

"That's why you're alive, Mr. Maston. Your curiosity keeps you alive." It gave me a funny feeling—to think people who weren't like Father could be dead. They could be walking around, but they could be dead.

Father said, "I don't know how alive I am, but I know I'm a romantic about poetry. Just like Peakie."

Jack turned to look at me again. "Which poets do you like best?"

"Keats and Shelley," I said. "But I like Keats best."

"Now that's funny," Jack said. "I do, too. I wonder why?"

"Maybe it's because Shelley sounds as if he knew he was a poet. And Keats, well Keats just writes poetry."

Jack hit the side of his head with his hand. "That's it! Of course, that's it! I take my hat off to you." And he did, only it was a cap, a grey wool cap. He was the first man I ever knew who wore a cap.

"If you know that, you must be a poet yourself," Jack said. "I hope you'll let me see your poems some day?"

"Why yes, thank you, I'd be glad to," I said. Why did I say that? I never have said a thing as prissy as that in my entire life. But it didn't make any difference. Jack smiled. He knew what I meant.

I'm right! I said to Jo. I wanted to shout it right out loud to her. I've always been right! When people like each other, they know without having to say a thing. They just know. It was funny. I really wanted to say when people love each other, but it came out like each other, instead. It didn't make any difference anyway. I couldn't find Jo.

Nine

I DIDN'T have time to worry about what had happened to Jo. I didn't even have time to change my clothes. We had to sit down at the table the minute we got home because Benny had to go into Kansas City—Willy needed some money—and Manuel was going to drive her in as soon as supper was over.

I ran into the bathroom downstairs and washed my face and hands and brushed my hair. When I ran into the dining room and started to pull out my chair, Mother said, "Just a minute, please. Turn around. You forgot to brush the back of your head again." She turned to Jack. "This child lives under the happy illusion that nobody is ever walking behind her."

When Manuel came in with the blue-and-white dish that's divided into little dishes to hold the different stuff he fixes to put on the curry, Mother said, "I don't know if you met Manuel this morning, Jack. Manuel Silva, this is Jack Taylor."

Jack stuck out his hand. "Hello, Manuel." Manuel had to put the dish down so he could shake hands with Jack.

Beatrice looked at me and rolled her eyes way up, the way she does every time we go to Fred Harvey's at the station and Mother calls the waitresses "sister."

Mother's called them that ever since she's been going to the Labour Temple. The first time I went there with her, I said thank you to somebody who held the door open for me. Mother was ahead of me—she's always ahead, she walks so fast. Mother turned around and said, "What did you say?"

When I told her, "I just said thank you to that gentleman," she leaned down and whispered, "Don't call them gentlemen. They don't like it. Call them men."

When Manuel brought the curry dish to me, I took some of everything but the coconut. I almost dropped the spoon when Jack said, "Peakie, don't you like coconut?"

I could only remember Mother's voice, at a counter in Emery Bird's, when Beatrice wanted to buy something. "Why do you want a boudoir cap? Next to a coconut cake, a boudoir cap is the tackiest thing on God's green earth." So I said, "Coconuts are tacky."

"Tacky?" Jack said. "They're not tacky. They're not sticky at all."

I looked at Father. "Peakie didn't mean it the way you use it, Jack. Here in the Middle West, tacky means the opposite of—of stylish, I guess."

"The boys who have to climb up the trees to get them would agree with you on that. It can be bloody hard work."

"You've seen them climbing the trees?" I asked Jack.

"Yes—when coconuts were part of the cargo for my ship and we docked at the islands to load them."

Cargo! I bet he'd loaded all the things in John Masefield's poem on his ship—the "ivory and apes and peacocks" and the "sandalwood, cedarwood, and sweet white wine"—that he'd been to all the places in the poem that I didn't know where they were, but I liked to say their names over and over again, whenever it started to get dark. They sounded so mysterious, especially "Quinquireme of Nineveh from distant Ophir." I'd ask Jack if he had been to Nineveh or Ophir, if I ever got a chance.

But the minute supper was over, Mother took Jack's arm. "There's a record I want you to hear, Jack," she said to him. "It's very American. It's 'Carry Me Back to Old Virginny.' Alma Gluck sings it. She sings it beautifully, perfectly beautifully," so I called Dutch and went up to my room and shut the door.

I didn't want to hear the record. It's very embarrassing to listen to music with other people around—I never know where to look. Anyway, I wanted to put something down in the Book before I forgot. I turned to the part marked "What Mothers Shouldn't Do" and wrote, "Don't do things you tell your daughters not to do, like don't make personal remarks." I was going to put down, "And remember, politeness is to do and say the kindest thing in the kindest way," which is another thing Mother says all the time, but I felt too sad to write any more. Maybe because I couldn't find Jo. I could feel her slipping away the first day I went to the convent, but I got so busy being unhappy, and then reading Shakespeare with Mother Jane, and then conjugating French verbs with Mère Clotilde, that I didn't think much about it. And I knew I could always find her here in my room when I wanted to. But since this morning and Jack, I didn't really want to find her, and that was the part that made me feel truly sad.

I'll always love Jo. She's my favourite person in any book I'll ever read. If I read one thousand books, she will always be my favourite person. But since this morning and Jack, she's gone back into the *Little Women* book, and she won't ever come out again.

I lay down on the window seat and looked at the stars outside the window. I was so sad that I felt like Elizabeth Barrett Browning, and I told Dutch to jump up by my feet so she could be Elizabeth Barrett Browning's dog, Flush. But Dutch is so big—she's about eighty times bigger than Flush—that she fell right off the seat and dragged me off with her. And, of course, right at that very minute there was a knock at the door, and I heard Jack say, "Peakie? Can I come in?"

I ran to the door and opened it so fast that we bumped into each other, but he was nice—he pretended we hadn't.

"Hello," he said. "What a fine room you've got! Hello, Dutch," and he patted Dutch on her head. She put her paws up on his shoulders.

"Watch out," I said. "She slobbers when she likes you. Get down, Dutch, get down." I dragged her by her collar to the door. "Go on, go on downstairs and see Binkie."

Jack said, "I was hoping you'd let me see your poetry."

"Oh, thank you," I said.

"Where do you hide it?"

"How do you know I hide it?"

"Well, with an older sister—and you a wise young woman—"

"You are wise, Jack. I do hide it—in a book."

"Which one?"

"*Missions and Missionaries in Old Japan.* Beatrice pretends she's read everything in the house, but I know she hasn't read that one—and she never will."

"I never will, either," Jack said.

"Me either." I took the book off the shelf and pulled out the papers with the poems on them. "I don't know which one to show you. They're all terrible," I said.

"I can't believe that," Jack said. "Read the one you have in your hand now."

"It's one I wrote when I got home after Mother and I had seen Nazimova—she's a Russian lady—in a moving picture."

"I'll sit over here," Jack said, "and you read it to me. Poetry's meant to be heard, like songs."

"I went to the movies
The other day
To see Nazimova.
I didn't want to go
For I was tired.
But when I saw her
I forgot
That I was tired.
And I forgot
The fat man next to me
And the woman

Chewing gum behind me.
And I just thought
That she—Nazimova—
Was somehow typical
Of life as it should be.
A sort of flaming, brilliant life.
But when
I went into the glaring street
Where rude men jostled
And the newsboys shrieked
Of the latest murder,
It seemed
A dream
Of life
As it should be.

"It's terrible," I said. "But it's so awful when you come out of a moving picture, especially if the sun is still out. That's why I said I was tired. I wasn't tired. And there wasn't a fat man or a lady chewing gum or any newsboys. I just said that."

"You needed them to establish your mood," Jack said.

"I did?"

"Of course. Poets do that all the time. I'll show you. Do you have any poems by A. E. Housman?"

"If he's in *The Oxford Book of English Verse* I do." I got it off the table and gave it to him.

Jack looked in the front, turned to a page. "His 'Epitaph on an Army of Mercenaries' is here. That's a fine bitter one, but I wanted to show you the one that starts, 'Loveliest of trees, the cherry now.' It's not here. No matter," he said. "I'll send it to you when I get back to England."

"You will?"

"I will, indeed. Or I'll have a friend send it. I may be in jail."

"What have you done?"

"It's more what I haven't done. I haven't registered for military service, and I won't. I'll go to jail first. Fighting and killing are evil. I'll have no part of them."

"They wouldn't put you in jail for that!"

"Wouldn't they just! Three of my friends are there right now."

"Don't go back," I said. "Stay here. We'll hide you."

Benny told me when a person drowns, in the second just before they go down for the third time, they see their whole life—everything that's ever happened to them. I never drowned, of course, so I don't know, and the people who have drowned couldn't tell anybody because they drowned, so how does anybody know that they see their whole life? But I know I can figure out a whole play, and what the scenery looks like and the costumes, and I can act it all out to the end. And when Benny comes in or calls me, I find out I've done it all in one minute. I started to figure out, when he said he might have to go to jail, how we could hide Jack.

I wouldn't tell Father or Mother. It would worry Father, and Mother would boast about it at the Labour Temple. I certainly wouldn't tell Beatrice—she'd use it as another chance to tease me about acting. She's uncanny that way—she always knows when I'm acting. The minute she walks in my room she says, "I'm sorry to interrupt the rehearsal, but Mother wants you." I would tell Benny—her grandmother had to hide in barns and cellars when she ran away from Alabama; that was before Abraham Lincoln—so she'll help. We could make a bed for him in the attic. It's cold in there, but Jack could come out and sit in my room or Benny's. And Benny and I could take turns being sentinels. If one of us saw a stranger coming up the walk, the other one would whistle "Yankee Doodle came to town" (I'd have to say it, because I can't whistle), and the other one would take Jack down the basement stairs and hide him in the storm cellar.

I was trying to figure what to tell the stranger to get his mind off asking what was on the other side of the storm-cellar door when Jack said, "That's very kind of you, Peakie, but I'm not going to get any of my American friends in trouble."

"How would anybody know you were here?"

"They probably already know. They checked on me at the I.W.W. camp. They'll deport me as an undesirable alien and ship me back to England. Then I'm in for it—if they catch me."

"Who are they?"

"Your government—or representatives of your government. Your government's very sympathetic towards the warmongers. The British warmongers. They'll have you in the war before long."

"Me?"

"Your country. They're working bloody hard at it—spreading propaganda to appeal to your sympathies or to persuade you that England's fighting a just war."

"It isn't a just war?" I asked him.

"There's no such thing as a just war." He sounded angry. "Don't listen to the warmongers. Or the statesmen. Or the generals."

"Who do you want me to listen to?" I asked. He came over and put his hand on my shoulder.

"Listen to your poets, Peakie. Listen to the writers who do their own thinking. Like Shaw. Like George Bernard Shaw. I'll send you his books when I get back. And Grenville Barker's. Oh, I'll send you a host of books. If you want to read them."

"I promise to read every single solitary word," I said.

"Good. I'll send them as soon as I get back, or I'll have a friend send them. And you write to me. I'll leave you my friend's address. You write to me what you think about them. I promise to answer every single solitary letter."

"Where will you be?"

"I have a friend on a trawler. He'll get me over to the continent if he can, and I'll ship out on a tramp steamer, and then—"

"Peakie, why didn't you answer me? I've been calling you until I'm blue in the face." Mother was standing in my doorway.

"My fault, Mrs. Maston," Jack said. "I hope she's not in trouble because I've been talking too much."

"She's in trouble," Mother answered, "but not because you talked too much—because she talked too much. That Mother Superior called—how do you pronounce her name, Peakie?" She turned to Jack. "We're spending thousands of dollars to have her learn French—she might as well pronounce it for me."

"Mère Bernadette," I said.

"That's it," Mother said. "Well, your Mère Bernadette just telephoned me and said that you had been very rude to her. She wouldn't tell me what you said. She said to ask you." Mother stood up very straight and folded her arms. "All right, I'm asking you. What did you say to her?"

"I told her I didn't want to say that poem in front of the curtain."

"What poem? In front of what curtain? You're making no sense at all."

"At the Christmas pageant. Mère Bernadette wanted me to come before the curtain, before they do the play in the stable, and she gave me the poem she wanted me to say."

"So what were you rude about?"

"I told her I didn't want to say it—"

"Why not?"

"Because it is a terrible poem."

"How do you know it's a terrible poem?"

"I just know."

"Well, now. I didn't realize until this very minute that you were Poet Laureate of Kansas City."

All at once I was mad. I was so mad that I could hardly see Mother. I don't know why it says in books, "He was so mad, he saw red." When I'm mad, I can hardly see at all —everybody gets blurry and I feel as if there was a lot of disgusting gravy in my mouth. Brown gravy, with lumps in it, that makes it hard to talk and makes me afraid I'm going to throw up.

I said, "I'm not going to say it," and I ran out of the room. I was halfway down the stairs before I remembered to stop, I was so mad, and listen.

"I don't know what we're going to do with that child."

That was Mother. "Beatrice is no problem at all. She's a sweet, lovely girl—she does what's expected of her. But Peakie! She's stubborn, she asks the damnedest questions, or you don't hear a peep out of her for days and then bang, she makes a declaration of independence. I don't know what's going to happen to her when she grows up."

"I'll be more interested in what happens to her when she grows up than what happens to Beatrice," Jack said. "Beatrice is a sweet, pretty girl. But that Peakie! She's got a touch of the rebel in her. It can lead her anywhere. I hope I'm around to see where."

I thought, I'm going to die. I'm going to die of happiness. Right here on the stairs. If I don't die of happiness, I will never forget this moment. I will remember this moment every minute, every hour, all the days of my life.

I never thought I would ever go to sleep, but I must have because Father was patting my shoulder and saying, "Wake up, dear. Wake up, Peakie."

I opened my eyes. "What's the matter? It's dark."

"It's very early. But if you want to say good-bye to Jack, you'd better get right up."

I started towards the chair with my clothes on it, but Father said, "There isn't time to get dressed. Jack wants to get down to the railroad yards while it's still dark."

I stumbled down the stairs after Father. Everybody was in the hall. Jack stood near the door. Mother was by him, with a sweater in her hands she was trying to make him put on. Father walked up to him. He tried to give him some money. "Please, Jack, so we won't worry about you riding the rods." Beatrice had a wool scarf a beau had given her. Manuel had a box—with food in it, I guess. I guess there was food in the paper bag Benny had, too.

"No, no!" Jack laughed. "You're incredibly kind people—all of you—but I mustn't let you. You'll soften me up."

He put on his cap. He doesn't see me, I thought. Just as if I'd said it out loud, he looked straight at me—walked over to the staircase. I was standing so many steps up, I could look straight into his eyes.

"I'll send the books," he said. "I won't forget." He gave me a big hug. I hugged him back. "You write to me everything you think," he said. "Don't forget."

"I won't," I said. I said it into his shoulder—it was hard, and it smelled like the tall grass behind the house after Manuel has cut it.

He stopped hugging me and turned back to the door. I ran up to my room, to the window seat, and looked out of the window. In a minute I saw Jack and Father come out and walk around to the Ford. They went around the corner and they were gone. I was crying so hard that I had to swallow to get my breath back. It wasn't like crying over a poem. I wanted to stop and I couldn't stop. I'd almost stop and then I'd think of him saying, "Don't forget," and I'd start again. It wasn't a bit the way Romeo said it was. Parting isn't such sweet sorrow at all. I must tell him that, I thought, and I got a handkerchief out of the top drawer and blew my nose and found a piece of clean paper and started to write my first letter to Jack.

Ten

FATHER decided to go to war, so I was going to Massachusetts. Mother didn't want to be out in Marlborough all by herself, so they decided to close it up and she was going to go to school with me.

"I bet I'll be the only girl at Westlake that has her mother with her," I told Father.

"Now, Peakie, she won't be at Westlake with you. She'll be down at a hotel in Shelton."

"I don't see why she can't stay here and weave until you get back."

"Weave?"

"Like the wife of that man in *The Odyssey* who kept weaving and then pulling it all out every night until her husband came home from the war."

"I don't believe your mother would care very much for weaving," Father said, and started to laugh. I had to laugh, too, even if I was mad at Mother. Mother can't sew on a button. But then I got mad again.

"Why does she have to stay in Shelton? Why can't she stay in New York? That's where I'd stay."

"New York is a very big city. It can seem too big when you're all by yourself."

"I won't think so. That's where I'm going to live when I grow up."

"Maybe you'll change your mind when you see it." Father looked at me. "Can you keep a secret?"

"Father, you know I can."

"Yes, of course I do. I'm sorry I said that." That's one of the reasons Father is so wonderful: he's the only grown-up person I know who ever says he made a mistake to his children. "All right. Get ready. You are going to see New York. In about four months. In December."

"This December? This December I'm going to see New York?" I jumped into his lap. I didn't care if I was almost fourteen.

I hugged him so hard he said, "Look out, you're breaking my neck! You and your mother and Beatrice are going to spend your Christmas vacation there. New York is going to be my Christmas present to you. I hope you won't be disappointed with it."

"Disappointed! How could I be disappointed? About New York? Thank you, Father, thank you, thank you, thank you," I said, and ran upstairs to tell Jack in a letter. About going to New York. And to Massachusetts. And about Father going to war. He wasn't going to fight. He's a Quaker. He doesn't go to a Quaker meeting house, but he thinks like a Quaker, Mother says, and Quakers don't believe in fighting. He was going to be the Red Cross man in a big hospital, the man who saw that the Red Cross did what it was supposed to do in the hospital.

And, of course, I had to tell Jack the way I felt about the last books his friend had sent me from London. I read every book Jack sent me or that he asked his friend to send me: he sent me the poems by A. E. Housman he'd promised to send, he sent stories by Thomas Hardy and Joseph Conrad, and plays by Henrik Ibsen and Oscar Wilde and John Galsworthy, and short stories by Anton Chekhov and Guy de Maupassant. Some of the books were already here on the shelves, but I never would have read them if Jack hadn't sent them to me.

The books came from London. Jack's letters came from a different place every time—places with mysterious names and romantic names, like Colombo, which is in Ceylon, and Shanghai, in China, and Capetown, at the end of Africa, and he'd tell me what they were like.

When he wrote from Gibraltar, which is an English place in the Mediterranean—he called it Gib: it's not a place, I guess, it's a big rock—he said, "I wish you were here to see Gib tonight. It looks heavenly in the moonlight. I've no doubt you'll see it some day, and let us hope the day will be soon. It will make you want to write poetry if you see it on a night such as this. I can't look at Gib now without being reminded of the thousands of poor English lads who have seen it for the first, and last, time as they sailed by it on their way to be butchered, sent to die, they didn't know why, by English capitalists, to be killed by German lads who didn't know why."

I didn't have much time to write to him. There was so much to do. *I* didn't really have very much to do, but Mother wanted me to go with her every day when she went out to close up Marlborough. We had moved into a big hotel on Main Street. Mother said it was run down since she was a girl. They used to go there for supper after they had been to the opera house—that's what she always calls the theatre when she talks about the old days. But I thought it was grand.

I loved going down to the big dining-room to have breakfast with Father. The coloured waiter—his name was Nicholas and he knew Father—called me Miss Peakie, and he pulled out my chair for me and unfolded the big white napkin and draped it over my lap. And Father let me order anything I wanted. I never ordered orange juice—I always expected to taste castor oil in it—but I had buttered toast, white buttered toast, and sweet rolls and doughnuts.

I loved going up and down in the elevator and running down the long corridors with the red carpets on them if nobody was around. And the clean sheets! Every day we had clean sheets. "I don't think I'll have a house when I get married. I'll live in a hotel," I told Father.

"That will be kind of hard on your eight girls."

"My eight boys." I had changed the eight girls to eight boys after being around all those babies in the convent.

"That's right. Your eight boys. They'll want a yard to play in. Boys, especially, want a lot of space."

I didn't tell him—I didn't want to hurt his feelings—but he was doing what he always tells me not to do. He was generalizing. I knew if they were my boys, they would love to grow up in a hotel. Anyway, I plan to be very rich and have a place in the country. Benny will stay out there with Willy—that will give him a job. The boys can go out there when they get tired of the hotel. It will be like the place in *Jo's Boys*—big and kind of run-down. It will look run down, but everything will work. It just won't look neat.

Mother was so neat that she drove everybody crazy closing up Marlborough. She didn't do anything herself. She sat downstairs in the dining room. She had covered the table with lists she had made and tags and labels.

"I am the Duke of Wellington," she said, "and you are my courier. Take this dispatch to Benny. She's my lieutenant in the attic."

I'd take a list up to Benny—she would check the linen on it, stuff we never used—and then I'd bring the list back to Mother, and she'd give me the tag for me to take back to Benny. It would have "Best Linens" written on it.

The first day I got so tired running up and down stairs that I flopped out flat on the dining-room floor.

Mother looked down at me and said, " 'Smiling, the boy fell dead.' "

We had to skip Marlborough when Miss Perkins came to the hotel to make my dresses for school. The sweaters and skirts that the catalogue said I had to have for daytime we got at Emery Bird's. And the blouses with the Peter Pan collars. "Why do they call them that?" I asked Mother. "Peter Pan never wore anything like that."

"You can ask him when you get to Kensington Gardens," Mother said. Miss Perkins was going to make the three informal dinner dresses that the catalogue said I had to have. Mother had her copy three from the pictures in *Little Women.* They were really beautiful.

"You'll have to brush the back of your head when you wear them," Mother said.

I hated to say good-bye to Benny, but she promised to write to me, and she'll come back when we get back. I didn't mind saying good-bye to Manuel. The worst was Dutch and Binkie. Father is giving them to Mr. McClintock, the man that has the nursery, and they won't come back. "It wouldn't be kind to them or to McClintock," Father said.

Mr. McClintock is the man who's going to help me to get rich. Jack underlined some words in a play he sent me. They said, "I wouldn't have money. I wouldn't be rich. I'd be too ashamed." Jack wrote that everybody who is rich is rich because they or their fathers didn't pay their workers enough money.

But the way I'll get rich won't be taking anything from anybody. I'm going to have a flower company, and I will deliver flowers to people's houses every week, just like the milkman comes with the milk. Mr. McClintock said I'd better give them a list of flowers so they can check off which flowers they like, and that's a very good idea. Think how mad I'd be if I got a bunch of those flowers that look as if they were made from the bristles on a brush and are orange, the very worst colour in the world. Orange is always the same—like that man at Father's Store who says every time he sees me, "Hello, Peakie. How you have grown." *Every time.* Calendulas—that's the name of them.

Beatrice is really and truly wrong about things not being the way they are in books—or moving pictures—or plays. The more things that happen to me, the more I know she's wrong. And if you know that what is happening to you is like a book—or a moving picture—or a play, it makes it more exciting.

The time between the time we left Marlborough and the time Mother and I were in Boston did go by so fast that it was just a blur, the way it says in books. It seemed as if one minute I was running up and down the stairs at Marlborough with lists and the next minute Mother and I were in a room in a hotel in Boston and Mother was taking her rope out of the suitcase. She's afraid of fires so she always carries a rope she can slide down in case there is a fire. I always beg her not to take it out until after the bellboy goes, and she always says, "I thought you were the girl who didn't care what people thought." But in the Boston hotel I didn't say anything—I watched her take the rope out and put it in a big circle by the window, and take out her kiki bowl and put it on the little table between our beds, and I didn't say anything.

Mother looked at me. "Where's Pavlov's dog?"

"What do you mean?" It was strange—I felt I had pulled the words all the way up from my heels. I could see them climbing up my leg, up the front of me. When they climbed up my throat and past my palate—that red thing hanging down like a stalagmite or a stalactite in that cave in the Ozarks with bats hanging on it—I thought, am I going to throw up?

When Mother asked the telephone girl to get the number of Father's Store, I lay down on the bed and listened.

"John," she said after a little while. "Are you all right, lamb? Is Hattie spoiling you the way she should? Yes, I'm all right, or I will be as soon as you tell me something. When you take a shower—they only had a room with a shower in it empty—when you take a shower, what do you do? Oh, fiddle. I know that, but after you turn the water on, what do you do? Do you put the soap on first and then get under the water, or do you get under it and then put the soap on? All right, I'll try your way. Yes, they got the tickets for *Maytime*—they were here when we got here. No musical can possibly be as beautiful as Beatrice says this *Maytime* is—she must have acquired a crush on the tenor. But we're going. If Peakie doesn't have a fever. She's acting as if she has a fever—it may only be excitement."

After she'd sent her love to Aunt Hattie and told Father how she missed him and all the rest she says before she says good-bye, she came over to the bed and felt my ears—that's the way to tell if anybody has a fever, Mother says. She doesn't know how to read a thermometer. "I can't see the red line you say you see, and I'm not going to spend the best years of my life looking for it."

"You do have a fever," Mother said. "We're not going to *Maytime*."

"I haven't any fever. I haven't. It's because I've still got my coat on. Please, please, Mother."

"We'll see." That expression! That is the absolute worst one she has. That has been in the Book for ages. "Take off your coat and go and wash your face. We'll go down to dinner. Then we'll see."

There wasn't any blur about the dinner or the dining-room. It was a big tall room, with dark red curtains and a dark red rug and very white tablecloths.

"The tablecloths are very white," I said to Mother.

"White is white. It can't be very white. Henry James wouldn't like to hear you say that. This is his home town. That may be Henry James's cousins sitting at the next table." Any time Beatrice or I ever say anything about anybody in a restaurant, Mother always says, "Hush, those may be her cousins at the next table." She never thinks maybe Beatrice or I would rather not have the waiter or the people at the next table hear all about us. She talks to waiters and waitresses and maids and porters and elevator boys as if she had known them a long time. That isn't like a book. The ladies in books say short things to servants like "Thank you," and "Bring in the tea now, will you, Wilkins?" Of course, we never have tea.

In Boston, when the man who led us to the table handed me a menu, it was as big as *The Kansas City Star* but stiffer. Mother looked at me over the edge of her menu and said, "Don't order Welsh rarebit." She looked up at the man. "I sent this child down one morning when we were on a trip to have breakfast by herself. She had just learned to read, but not very well—because she ordered a Welsh Rarebit. She thought it was Welsh Rabbit and that they would bring her a little white rabbit—in a basket, I suppose, to play with."

She laughed. I looked up at the man, and he was smiling. If once, just once, a waiter or a maid or a porter, anybody, wouldn't think Mother was funny, maybe she'd stop embarrassing me.

"What do you want?" Mother asked. "If you can't have a rabbit?"

I didn't want anything, but I didn't want her to know that.

"Now don't tell me you can't read the menu—after all the thousands we spent on the French convent."

Chicken—white chicken—was all I could think of eating. Chicken on white bread, so I said, "I want a chicken sandwich."

"Come to the Touraine and order a chicken sandwich!" Mother said, but she ordered it for me with a glass of milk she knew I wouldn't drink. Beatrice told me when I was little that milk was ground-up chalk with water poured over it. I've never been able to drink it. Just like she told me I'd get a new set of teeth every year, so I didn't wash my teeth, I just wet my toothbrush. When Mother caught me doing it, she said, "If you're enough of a ninny to believe such a silly story, you deserve to have yellow teeth." I remembered that when I was sitting in the Touraine and thought I must put in the Book, "Be careful what stories your children hear." There was that little girl who lived in the house behind Gampie's who told me if I swallowed a cat's hair, a cat would grow in my stomach, and I've hated cats since she told me.

I felt too funny to eat, but Mother didn't notice. She clutched my arm. "Don't make it obvious, but look at that girl coming in the door."

There was a girl all in black standing in front of a man and woman, waiting. Mother whispered, never taking her eyes off the girl, "That's Marilyn Miller."

"Do you know her?"

"Of course I don't know her."

"Then how do you know who she is?"

"Because I read something besides *Little Women.* If you had ever read *The New York Times* once, you would know her name. She is a lovely dancer. Her husband just died, poor thing."

I was sorry Marilyn Miller's husband had died, but I was glad she had come to dinner where we were because Mother kept her head turned to look at her so I could sneak the chicken sandwich down my collar inside my panty waist. I couldn't have eaten it. I had to see *Maytime.* I had to. I'd die if I didn't see it.

I did see *Maytime*—part of it—and it was beautiful. It was so beautiful and so sad! When the lady, in a dress like the dress Queen Victoria has on in the picture in my room—all white, with a big skirt with roses on it, but the lady didn't look like Queen Victoria because Queen Victoria's eyes pop out and she's got a tiny little mouth and this lady was beautiful—when she sang a song to her friend, a soldier who had to go away, "Sweetheart, sweetheart, sweetheart, Will you love me ever? . . . To life's last faint ember, Will you remember?", I started to cry and I couldn't stop. It was awful. I sat there, and I listened to myself cry.

Mother tried to stop me. First she whispered, "Hush!" Then she said out loud, "Hush! Hush!" I didn't stop. I couldn't. She turned towards me in the dark. "Now mind me. Hush! Or I'm going to take you back to the hotel."

I couldn't hush. We went back to the hotel. I kept on crying all the way there and up in the elevator, while I got undressed, while I got in bed.

When I heard Mother say, "Wake up, Peakie, wake up. It's time to go to school," I opened my eyes and it was morning, and Mother was standing there all dressed.

I guess I got dressed—I must have because suddenly we were on a train, and Mother was saying, "Look out of the window. See the stone walls? This is the country your father likes."

"This is the weather the cuckoo likes," I said, "and so do I."

Mother gave me a funny look, but she didn't say anything. I went to sleep—I think. I was back in the blurry part of the book again. The blur went away when a taxicab we were in stopped in front of a big, dark red house. It looked like Gampie's house, only it was short and spread out like Aunt Hattie, and Gampie's house was tall and thin, like Mother. There were girls standing in bunches talking on the porch by the door. They stopped talking when Mother took hold of the edge of her cape and waved it like a big black-and-white flag at the taxi driver. "Please put the bags up there, Friend," she said. "Come on, Peakie, come on. 'Damn the torpedoes'—full speed ahead." I heard giggles as we walked through the door.

We walked into a dark hall. That had a lot of girls in it, too. I pulled on Mother's cape.

"What do you want, Babe? Stop pulling at my cape." I never knew how clear her voice was.

"Mother," I whispered, "don't talk."

"What do you mean, don't talk?"

"Just don't talk." I'll disappear, I thought. I'll walk out of the door and disappear. Nobody can stop me from turning around and walking out of the door.

Mrs. Conway stopped me. That was the name of the lady who walked up to us. She really ran up to us. She must run all the time—maybe that was why she was so thin, as thin as Mother—and she didn't stop running when she got to us. She kind of ran in place. And her hands fluttered around when she talked. Mother uses her hands a lot when she talks, but they don't flutter; they fly straight in front of her or they swoop, but they don't flutter.

Mrs. Conway and Mother talked. I stood there and thought, I've got to lie down. Mrs. Conway called, "Susan, dear," and one of the girls who had been listening came over.

"Susan, this is Peakie Maston. This is Susan Perry. Will you take Peakie to her room? She's going to have the room at the end of Corridor West." She turned to Mother. "Peakie was entered so late, Mrs. Maston, we've put her in a room by herself. The girls chose their roommates last term—or have been assigned to roommates. Perhaps later—"

Mother said, "That's all right. That's perfectly all right. Peakie likes to 'wander lonely as a cloud'."

Mrs. Conway looked at Mother. "Of course," she said. Susan said, "Come on." I started to follow her.

Mother called out, "Aren't you going to say good-bye to your Mother Machree?"

I turned back. Mother put her arms around me. She sang in a whisper, but everybody could hear her, "To life's last faint ember, Will you remember?"

I broke away from her and ran up the stairs.

Susan came running after me. "Hey, what are you doing? You don't know where to go." She had a funny way of talking. Father says you shouldn't say things are funny because they are different. So I guess I should say she had a different way of talking. Her a's sounded different from the way we said a's in Kansas City. I thought she was going to be nice—she smiled at me when we got to my room. She smiled when she said, "There's not much room in here to 'wander lonely as a cloud,' Babe. This used to be a maid's room. You don't have maids out West, do you? You do your own chores, don't you, Babe?" She smiled when she said, "Your mother's crazy, isn't she?"

I should have hit her. But I didn't. Suddenly I saw Marlborough—it was little, like a house inside a candy Easter egg, but clear. I could see Benny come out on the porch. I could hear her call, "Dutch! Binkie! Come on in and eat. Don't you dogs keep me standing here, holding this door open and letting all the flies in. Come on, now." And I fell back on the bed and started crying.

"Oh, for Pete's sake! Another sniffler!" Susan said. She slammed the door as she went out.

The tears were running into my ears. It was uncomfortable, but I didn't care. I didn't care about anything. I just wanted to go back to Marlborough and go to sleep.

I did go to sleep. I didn't wake up until I felt somebody shake me. I opened my eyes. The room was dark. In the light from the hall, I could see it was a maid who was shaking me.

"The dressing bell has rung, miss," she said. "Shall I turn on the lamp?"

I must have said yes, because the room got bright, too bright—it hurt my eyes. But I tried to be polite. "What is your name? My name is Peakie."

"Rose, miss. You really should get up. You'll be late."

"You're Irish, aren't you?" I asked her. "I can tell. You talk like Molly Lenihan. She's Irish. She's a friend of mine. You're prettier than she is, and she's a lot older than you are, but—"

Rose said, "You really must get dressed, miss. Let me help you." She opened the door to the closet. Somebody must have unpacked my things while I was asleep, for I could see the skirts hanging up and the three *Little Women* dresses.

"Oooh," Rose said. "I've never seen dresses like them! They're all so grand! Which one do you want to put on, miss?"

I pointed at the Jo one. Jo's was red, not mitten red but red like the ruins of Pompeii that are in the picture on my wall at Marlborough, and it had two ruffles around the skirt and one around the sleeves. And a white collar with a black velvet bow in front. And white sleeves that came out from under the red part of the sleeves. A bell rang while I was trying to make the hooks go into the eyes.

"I'll help you, miss," Rose said, and finished the line of

them just like that. "Hurry down now. You're looking grand!"

I started down the stairs. I felt dizzy. I held onto the banister. I heard voices—I could see girls standing in a big room. When I got to the hall, I walked in. Everybody stopped talking. Everybody stopped moving. Everybody looked at me.

Mrs. Conway looked at me. She called, "Come in, come in, Peakie. Come in and meet all—"

"I forgot to brush the back of my head," I said, and I turned and started to run up the stairs. I had to stop and sit down on a step, I was so dizzy. I heard the giggling again.

I felt somebody's hand on my head, heard somebody say, "Why, she's burning up!" That's all I did hear.

I never did get upstairs to brush the back of my head.

Eleven

I ALMOST died in the infirmary—that's what they call a hospital in boarding school. I had Spanish influenza—it was something new, and it was making people, and the soldiers, too, die all over the place.

At least, Mother said I almost died, but you have to watch her: she'll say anything to make what happens sound more exciting. I must have been awfully sick, anyway. I don't know how I got to the infirmary. I know I had terrible dreams when I got there. They were always happening in a cave that was dark red where it wasn't black in the corners. My hands felt swollen up as big as my head, and I kept bumping them into dark red rocks and hurting them. I was looking for somebody. I don't know who I was looking for. Maybe it was Jo, because I woke up for one minute and I could hear somebody say, but I couldn't see who said it—it was like listening in on a party line on the telephone—"She keeps saying Jo. Is Jo the name of her beau?"

And then Mother's voice, "Don't be ridiculous! The child's never even met a boy!"

I wanted to get on the party line, too, and say, "Don't tell her about the rabbit," but I couldn't. I'd started to go back into the dark red cave again.

The next time I woke up Mother was standing by my bed. "Mama," I said, "I never saw you with an apron on."

"You're still quite delirious, dear child, quite," Mother said in her imitation English accent. "I'm not your mama. I am Florence Nightingale." She had a piece of cloth that was wet, and she wiped my face with it. It felt lovely. She took hold of my hand and said, "Go back to sleep, baby," and she started to sing, "Go tell Aunt Rhody, go tell Aunt Rhody, go tell Aunt Rhody, the old grey goose is dead." She had taught it to me to sing to my dolls when I was little, even though, she told me, I couldn't carry a tune from here to the garage. She smiled at me while she sang. I must put that in the Book, I thought, before I forget. Smile at your children—because Mother standing there singing Aunt Rhody and smiling was the most beautiful thing in the whole wide world.

It was good I didn't put it in the Book, because when I began to stay awake more, I saw that Mother was smiling at everybody in the infirmary, and it was jammed with other girls. They called her Miss Nightingale. When it was nighttime, she went around the beds carrying a lamp with a candle inside it. "Historically, it's incorrect," she'd say. "I had to get a Paul Revere lamp—they were out of Florence Nightingale ones in the village." And she smiled at all of the girls in bed. And all of them were crazy about her.

There were only two nurses to take care of everybody,

on account of the war, Mother said, and the people dying like flies from the Spanish influenza. That was the awfullest expression—dying like flies. If people really saw what they said, if when they said dying like flies, they saw a big bunch of flies buzzing against a screen, and when somebody pumped that spray at them, they saw them dropping off the screen, down in a heap, with some of them turning over and some of them buzzing right up to the last minute, they'd never say dying like flies again. Not in front of somebody who was sick anyway.

The nurses were crazy about Mother, too. And Dolores, she was a girl from Spain—she'd come all the way from Spain to learn English at Westlake—she would start clapping her hands before Mother even got to her bed. Mother always took off her apron when she got there and twirled it around like a bullfighter does and said, "Olé!" and sang, "Toreador, dumpty-tee, dumpty-tee, dum," to her. I thought it was silly. It was so obvious. But Dolores loved it.

Even Susan Perry was crazy about her. When Mother found out that Susan came from New York, she sang "East Side, West Side" when she was changing the sheets on Susan's bed. And she called Susan Rosie O'Grady and told her, "When you get well, you can go home and 'dance the light fantastic on the sidewalks of New York'." Now that was really silly, because I just happened to know that Susan lived in a big house on Fifth Avenue, and I bet she never danced anything on the sidewalks of New York in her entire life.

When she and I got better, we sat out in the sun on a

porch with windows around it. Susan said, "You are so lucky! Your mother's absolutely divine!" She said it in her la-dee-da New York voice.

I turned my chair so I could look straight at her. "You don't think she's crazy?"

"Don't be absurd. Of course I don't think she's crazy."

"You said she was crazy."

"You're crazy! I never said she was crazy." Susan was lying. She did remember she'd said it, and she knew I knew she remembered, because she did what people always do when they know people know they're lying. She started to talk very fast and in a voice that was higher than her regular voice. "I'm so jealous of you. Your mother is such fun. My mother is so serious. She's on so many boards and committees and things. She's always having to go to the hospital or to the club—"

"Do they have clubs just for ladies?"

"Of course." Susan got back her regular voice. "But of course, you wouldn't know. They probably have never heard of clubs out West."

"We don't live out West. We live in Kansas City."

"Father says anything west of the Hudson is the West." She pronounced Father like Faather.

"Well, your father is crazy. Kansas City is right in the middle of the Middle West."

"Oh, well, that's even worse. All those hogs and corn. And isn't Kansas where the Ozarks are? Where you never wear any shoes?"

"We live in Kansas City, Missouri. We don't live in Kansas City, Kansas. And we don't have any hogs." Father had tried to grow corn in the field behind Marlborough, but I wasn't going to tell Susan that. "And I've always had millions of shoes—millions of shoes. And we do too have clubs. Father takes me to lunch all the time at the University Club. And ladies go there when they give big lunches. Mother never goes to them—she says she'd never hear any talk at them as good as what she can read in Henry James—and besides, if she went, she'd have to get dressed. I suppose you think that's crazy."

Susan got back her high voice. "I don't think it's crazy at all. I think it's—it's quaint."

Quaint! I could hardly wait to tell Beatrice. Every time we pick up something in a store, something that is pretending to be something else, like a bell pretending to be an old-fashioned lady with a bonnet and a full skirt, Mother always says, "Never in my house. It's quaint."

Susan went on, "I'm absolutely serious. I'm so jealous of you. Imagine having someone like your mother around. It must be like having a moving-picture star in your house all the time."

I wanted to tell her that sometimes you get sick of having a moving-picture star around all the time. Sometimes you'd like to have a mother around that's like the mothers in books, not beautiful, but pleasantly plump, with a kind, cheerful face—that's the way they always describe them—who sews pretty dresses at night to surprise you with in the morning and who takes cookies with a spicy aroma out of the hot oven when you come in from sledding.

And who keeps still. Who keeps still so you can be the star sometimes. But I didn't tell her. I wasn't going to have any la-dee-da ninny making fun of any of us. I wouldn't lie to her. Beatrice lies to Mother sometimes to keep from fighting with her. I don't lie—I'm never going to lie—but I keep still sometimes to keep from fighting with her. If I don't feel like fighting.

I didn't feel like fighting with anybody for a long time at the infirmary. I didn't feel sick any more, but I felt as if I didn't have any bones in me. "Like a piece of tired celery," Mother said. And for once, she was right. I had to stay at the infirmary and sleep with an ironing board under my mattress because my back was weak. They sent lessons over for me to do, but they were kind of confusing without somebody to explain them, so I just slept and looked out at the leaves turning to red and orange and yellow, and thought about that story O'Henry wrote about that sick girl in New York who told a painter she'd die when the last leaf fell off the tree outside her window, so he climbed up and painted a leaf on the wall and she didn't die. I felt too much like celery to read any new stories.

Until one morning. The minute I woke up that morning I felt different. I felt as if a stream of water, clear water like the water in the stream in Colorado, was rushing very fast up and around and all through me. I jumped up and looked out the window. It had snowed during the night. The sun was out—it made diamonds in the snow. I put on my outdoor clothes and ran out of the door. I ran up to a big pine tree. The snow had put long white gloves on the green branches. I felt so different that I reached up and shook the lowest branch so the snow was all over me. I filled my mittens with snow, and I threw snow way up in the air. I sang out loud, "Allons, enfants de la patrie, le jour de gloire est arrivé!" and I didn't give a hoot in Harry that I couldn't carry a tune from here to the garage!

I didn't keep on feeling like that when I went back to school and my room on Corridor West. Father says that every day is like writing a page in your autobiography —he says when he remembers that, it sometimes stops him from doing something mean or petty that he wouldn't like to read in his autobiography later or have me and Beatrice read. I know he must feel that way—Father never lies—but I always feel more as if I were acting in a moving picture.

At Westlake, after the infirmary, I wasn't acting in the moving picture. I was in the dark moving-picture house watching the picture. I didn't write Father about it because you're only supposed to write cheerful news to soldiers in the war. He isn't exactly a soldier, and the war is over, but he's still over there, and he's going to stay there until all the soldiers in the hospital get well or are put on ships that will bring them home, but I still knew it would make him sad if I wrote to him that I was watching the moving picture and wasn't acting in it.

By the time I got back from the infirmary, all the girls who hadn't had best friends left over from last year had made best friends with the new girls. They weren't mean to me. They said "Hello" and "Good night" and all the regular things, but in free periods they didn't invite me into their rooms, so I stayed in my room and read the books Jack sent me. Dinner was the bad time. I knew the first night I got back that the dresses Miss Perkins had copied from

Little Women were all wrong. The rest of the girl's dresses were made of taffeta in pink or blue, or they were velvet dresses with lace collars. None of them had full skirts like the *Little Women* dresses.

I knew the first night that I talked wrong, too, when I said supper instead of dinner and called the maid a lady. You're not supposed to call anybody a lady, except a Lady-lady, like Lady Hamilton. So I didn't talk at all except to say "Please" and "Thank you." I'd go down to Mother's hotel for lunch on Saturdays and Sundays, but Miss Bridges was always there for lunch, too. She was a new friend Mother had met. She was mixed up in some new religion, and I hated her. She looked all the time as if she were thinking beautiful thoughts and she needed to have her hair washed.

I had to be nice to her because Mother said she was helping her find spiritual comfort, and I guess Mother needed spiritual comfort with Father in France and worrying about him over there.

But Mother acted different around Miss Bridges. She didn't swear or make the waitresses laugh, and it scared me to see Mother different. Miss Bridges was what was making her different, and I hated her.

I certainly wasn't in the moving picture when the scenes were in the classes. I was there at a desk in the class, but the teachers never called on me. All of us who had been sick in the infirmary were so far behind the rest of the class that we were going to have to be tutored after school as soon as we were strong enough, and all next summer, too, so the teachers didn't ask us any questions.

When I asked a question in history class, Miss Whittemore—she was the history teacher and she had red hair and rode horseback when she wasn't teaching—when I asked her after she'd read us a long chapter about the English heroes of the Crusades, "How do you know that that was true?" she said:

"It's true because it's written in this history book."

"That doesn't make it true because it's in a book," I said. "Jack told me authors put in books what they think is true."

"This book happens to have been written by an eminent historian. It would be a little arrogant to doubt his veracity."

"He might be prejudiced," I said. " 'You have to keep using your faculty for doubting all the time.' That's what Jack said Anatole France said. He said the faculty for doubting is rare among men. Jack says to question and doubt everything. He says—"

"I don't know who Jack is," Miss Whittemore said. "And I'm not particularly interested in finding out. Please go to Mrs. Conway's office. After I've written a note for you to take."

Mrs. Conway wasn't cross at me after she read the note. She fluttered her hands, and she talked about not arguing with the teachers because they'd been to college and they knew all about their subjects, and about not asking why things were the way they were—just to be a sensible girl and know that they were the way they were because that's the way they were.

So I didn't ask any more questions. I didn't read any of

the books the teachers said I had to read either. When I have my eight boys, I'm not going to send them to school. I'm going to find a friend for them like Jack. They'll like him so much that they'll read every word in the books he gives them, even the hard parts, just the way I do. And if they didn't understand something or if they wanted to use their faculty for doubting, they could always write to him and ask him, and he'd always answer their letters. Maybe he could come and live with us—then they wouldn't have to write to him. They could ask him.

I wrote to Jack all the time. Jack and Father, too, of course, but I wrote to Jack more than Father because I had promised him I'd write to him everything I thought about the books he sent.

And I could tell him how boring school was, that there was only one class that was funny, the singing class, because after the first day when I sang out loud and Miss Ransome stopped playing the piano and said, "Who sang an E flat there? There's no E flat indicated," I never sang again. I stood there and moved my mouth while everybody else practised "Blow, blow, breathe and blow! Wind of the Western Sea." And Miss Ransome never knew. It would have been more fun if I could have laughed about it with somebody else. But I couldn't tell Father how boring school was. It would have hurt his feelings.

It was so boring that if it hadn't been for Father's letters and Jack's letters and the books Jack sent, I think I would have run away from school. The letters and the books, and knowing I was going to see New York at Christmastime. I wanted to wait and see how wonderful New York was before I ran away.

Twelve

IT WAS the most wonderful place in the whole wide world! New York was more wonderful than the pictures in the Scribner magazines—and in the Harper magazines—the ones in the attic at Marlborough! I don't know how I'm going to do it, with Jack and London and the eight boys and the house in the country I promised Benny, where Willy could stay, and the flower business I promised to be a partner in with Mr. McClintock, but I am going to New York, and I'm going to live there for the rest of my life. I'll figure out something. I am not going to invite Mother. She can come to visit me, but she's going to have to stay inside the house the whole time she's there.

I've already picked out the house where I'm going to live. It's nowhere near the hotel where we stayed at Christmastime. It's the house Mark Twain used to live in, and it's right on Fifth Avenue. Mother pointed it out to me when she took me for a ride in the snow on top of a bus that went all the way down Fifth Avenue.

There was just one other person riding up on top of the bus, a man with a black hat like my beaver hat, only smaller and turned up on one side, and a cane. When Mother grabbed my arm and said, "Look, there's Bonwit Teller's. That's where Gammie got her seal coat. When you buy your furs, always buy them at Bonwit Teller's," the man turned around and looked at me. I had on my beaver hat with Gammie's square silver belt buckle that Miss Perkins had sewed on the crown—"my Pilgrim hat," Mother called it—and my brown Harris tweed coat that was a boy's coat, but that was all right, Mother had said when we bought it at Emery Bird's, because I'm going to have to wear tailored things all my life—that's the kind of girl I am. The man looked at me and smiled.

I knew what he was thinking. I knew exactly what he was thinking. He was thinking that big square girl with that square face and those big feet and hands is never going to wear any furs.

Of course, I knew he was wrong. When I grow up, I won't be big and square. I'll be divinely tall, like Trilby—she had big feet and everybody was in love with her—and my face won't be square when I get to be a lady. It will be long and delicate like Lillian Gish's if I have to stay up every night and pull it up and down. I'll wear a veil, and I'll have a long black fur coat with a big muff to match, and I'll pin a bunch of white violets on the muff. But the man couldn't know that.

Mother grabbed my arm. "There's Scribners! They're the ones who publish dear Henry James." She laughed. "I went in there one time when I was here and told the first salesman that walked up to me that I came in because I was in love with Henry James."

"Oh, Mother," I said. The man had turned around again. "Didn't he think you were crazy?"

"Certainly not," Mother said. "He was very interested. We got to talking about Henry James, and the next thing you know, he telephoned and the man who was Henry James's editor came and took me to his office, and we talked and he showed me a letter from Henry James." Mother reached up and brushed some snow from her Cossack hat. "Afterwards his editor took me to tea. At Sherry's."

"Well, I'll be damned!" the man said.

"It's quite possible," Mother said. "But in the meantime, please stop eavesdropping on my conversation."

"I'll try not to, Madame," the man said. "But it's going to be difficult. Very difficult," and he turned back in his seat.

People were always eavesdropping on Mother. Every time we went to a restaurant, and we went to a different one every night so we could taste food from a different country every night, people eavesdropped.

I was the most embarrassed when we went to eat French food at the Hotel Brevoort and Mother wanted me to talk French to the waiter, and told him how many thousands of dollars they had spent to send me to the French convent and how stubborn I was when I wouldn't talk French with him.

Beatrice thought the worst time was when the waiter at the German food place said, after he gave us the menus, "Everything here is good—just like home cooking," and

Mother said, "Let's go, children. I can't bear home cooking. I don't have home cooking at home."

And when Beatrice said, "Oh, Mother, they'll think you're a tourist," Mother said, "Who do you think I am? Mrs. Astor's horse?"

The only meals I really liked were when Mother called "Room Service" and we ate in Mother's room, because after the waiter had taken all those silver hats off the food, we could eat and know that there wasn't anybody around to eavesdrop when Mother said something embarrassing.

If there weren't any people to eavesdrop when we first walked in some place, they came in after we'd been there a while. Mother took us to an elegant shop—"elegant enough for Mrs. Chandler Phelps Smith," Mother said. "She was so elegant, she wouldn't open a door for herself—she had a maid around to open it for her. She didn't have them around very long."

All they sold at this place, Tappé's, were hats.

Tappés's was only one room, with three little tables with mirrors behind them, and little chairs in front of the tables, but it looked very elegant.

There was only one lady when we got there. The lady was almost fat. She had straight black hair that was pulled up tight into a knot on the top of her head. She had on a black wool dress, a plain black dress with no pin or anything on it, but she looked elegant, too. "Yes, Madame?" she said to Mother.

"How do you do?" Mother said. "Have you seen *The New York Hat?*"

I wanted to leave right then, but Mother had hold of my arm. Beatrice walked to a window, pushed the long blue curtains back, and looked out at the street. She always knows how to get away. The lady had that surprised look on her face that people always get when Mother first starts talking, but by the time Mother had told her what a wonderful moving picture *The New York Hat* was, and how dear Mary Pickford was in it, and how kind Lionel Barrymore was, and how the lady must go to see it if they ever brought it back to New York because she would love it so, and she would understand why Mother couldn't let her daughters come to New York without getting a real New York hat for them, the lady was smiling and saying, "Bien sûr, Madame," and "Entendu," and "Ça va sans dire," and opening big drawers that were in the wall.

Mother called Beatrice to sit down in front of one of the little tables, and Henriette—she told Mother to call her that. "I insist, Madame," she said—put hats on Beatrice. She oohed and aahed every time she put one on. Beatrice sat there. She didn't say a thing until Henriette brought out a pink-rose hat. It was flat like a platter in the front, but the back was all roses, beautiful little pink and rose-coloured roses. Beatrice looked at herself in the mirror. "I like this one," she said.

"You'd be as crazy as old Mrs. Helm if you didn't," Mother said. "It makes you look as if you'd just stepped out of a picture by Watteau."

"Ah, Watteau!" Henriette shrieked. "Madame is so

right. I would love to have the girls see it on Mademoiselle. Madame permits?"

"Of course," said Mother. "You do look like a Watteau, Beatrice. You look lovely, perfectly lovely."

When the three girls, only they were women, came in, they said the same thing, in French, so Beatrice took the pink hat.

Mother said, "Now we need a hat for Peakie."

Henriette looked at me. "Something simple, yes?"

"Something simple yes," Mother repeated. "Yes, indeed. Take off your hat and sit down, Peakie." I took off my beaver hat and sat.

Henriette opened a drawer and pulled out a big black hat, a big plain black hat. It had nothing on it but a big black feather that stood up on one side. A plain big black feather. Henriette put it on my head, stood back, and clapped her hands. "Ça y est!" she shrieked.

"It is right. It's exactly right," Mother said.

I said, "I don't like it."

"Why not?" Mother asked.

"I want a hat with flowers on it."

Henriette and the girls, the women, went "non, non, non." This was the hat for la petite, they said—and other things I didn't know enough French to understand.

Beatrice was really mean. She stopped looking at herself in the long mirror between the windows to say, "Get it for her, Mother. She looks like one of the men in Rembrandt's 'The Night Watchmen.' "

" 'The Night Watch,' Beatrice," Mother said—at least

Beatrice hadn't said it right—but Mother got the hat for me. If I do have girls instead of boys and they want a hat that makes them look like a Watteau lady instead of a Dutchman watching, I'll get it for them. I don't have to write that down in the Book. I'll remember.

Sometimes the eavesdroppers hushed Mother. They hushed her when she took us to hear Caruso in *Pagliacci*. We climbed and climbed until we stood right up under the ceiling of the Metropolitan Opera House. The gold curtains opened up on the stage. It was so far away, I could hardly see the singers, but I could hear the music, and it made me homesick. It sounded exactly the way it sounded on the Victrola in the back room at Marlborough. Suddenly Mother clutched my arm. "There he is!" she cried. "There he is!"

"Where?" I asked her.

"Standing over there," and she pointed. "There in the wings. The one in white. There's Caruso!"

"That little white thing?" I said.

"That little white thing!" Mother yelled.

Beatrice said, "Oh, please, Mother," and started to walk away.

" 'Oh, please, Mother,' " Mother said. "I bring you to New York and take you to hear Caruso, and all you say is, 'Oh, please, Mother!' " but you could hardly hear what she was saying because people were yelling "Silence!" and "Silencia!" and other things I didn't understand at her. Some of them stood up and shook their fists. Mother said, "Hush. There he is!" and everybody hushed, even Mother.

She took us to the theatre every night. I got so tired that I went to sleep at some of the plays, but I didn't go to sleep when we saw "Justice" because it was a play that John Galsworthy wrote that Jack had sent me and because the most beautiful man I had ever seen, John Barrymore, was Falder. Falder was a clerk who stole a little money to help the lady he loved, and he was going to put it back, but they caught him and hounded him, so he committed suicide. He was another victim of the capitalistic system, Jack said.

That was one time I was proud of Beatrice. She hardly ever cries, but she started crying as soon as I did, and she kept on crying after the play was over. She walked up the aisle crying, and when a man said to her, "Don't cry, young lady. It's only a play," Beatrice wasn't one bit embarrassed.

She looked straight back at him and said, "It's not just a play. It's Life." She kept on crying all the way to the Astor.

When Mother and I came down from Boston and met Beatrice in the lobby of the Astor, she had barely said "Hello" before she got what Mother calls her Eastern look—she does it by turning away from you and looking into the corner of whatever room she's in—and said to Mother, "Why in heaven's name did you pick the Astor? Nobody I know ever stays at the Astor."

Mother snapped back at her, "I didn't pick it in heaven's name. I picked it because it's smack in the middle of Broadway, and I've got tickets for the theatre every night. And I know a great many people who stay here. I know Al Jolson and D. W. Griffith and—"

"Oh, please, Mother," Beatrice said. She looked at me. "Will you ask at that desk if there's any mail for me?"

"You see?" Mother said to her. "It doesn't make any difference what hotel we stay at as long as the mailmen know where it is. All you need is a place to wait for the mail."

Beatrice did ask a lot of times if there were any letters for her—and a lot of times there were letters. Somebody was in love with her again. She's been in love, or somebody has been in love with her, for years and years. Some of the ones who were in love with her or she was in love with I never saw.

The one who was in love with her when we were at the Astor was named Jake something. He lived in Texas. He must have been very rich because the first day we got there, he sent her such an enormous box of flowers that it took two bellboys to bring it up to our room.

"Good God," Mother said when they walked in with the box. "It's as big as a coffin."

"Please, Mother," Beatrice said. "Don't be vulgar."

"Let's not talk about being vulgar," Mother said. "That thing must hold enough flowers to satisfy Lillian Russell. Unless Jake's sent you a long-horn calf."

There wasn't any calf in it, of course. There were orchids. There must have been orchids of every colour, every kind that there were in the world. Beatrice took the card that was on top and walked over to a window. She smiled as she read it—she was acting as if she got a coffin of orchids every day—but her hands were trembling. That's the trouble when you act a lot yourself: it's very easy to see when other people are acting.

"All right, Lillian," Mother said. "Stop mooning over

that card and start figuring out what you're going to do with all these orchids."

Beatrice gave a start—she really is a terrible actress. "Why, I'm going to keep them, of course."

"There aren't enough vases in the city of New York, let alone at the Astor, for all those orchids," Mother said. "And I have no intention of living in a South American jungle for a week because you've got a crazy rancher for a beau."

Beatrice came over and looked down at the box. "There are an awful lot of them. What can we do with them?"

"I'll call the housekeeper," Mother said. "She can give them to the maids and the bellboys—the ones who have wives. Pick out the ones you want to keep first."

Beatrice picked one kind to wear for every day we were going to be in New York. When she said to Mother, "Now it's your turn," Mother said, "Thank you very much, but I never wear flowers—you know that. I can't bear to watch them die."

Beatrice was nice. She gave me a turn to pick, not ones to wear—I was too young for orchids, she said—but ones to put in a vase. I picked a spray of little lemon-coloured ones—they looked like butterflies flying. They made me decide to wear lemon-coloured orchids on my muff instead of white violets when I grew up.

Mother had an awful time getting the housekeeper. When she asked for her, the operator must have asked her why she wanted her, because Mother said, "I can't explain over the phone why I want her. No, I don't want another pillow. No, I don't want another blanket. I want the housekeeper. Just stop trying to read my mind, young woman, and send the housekeeper up here."

When the housekeeper came, she looked all ready to be cross—her mouth was shut into a little circle—but when Mother showed her the box of orchids and told her to take her pick and give the rest away, she was so excited that she almost made a curtsy before she took the box out of the door. She must have given an orchid to every single person who worked at the Astor, because for the whole week we were there, we couldn't order anything from a waiter, or ride in an elevator or pass a maid in the hall without their saying, "Thank you for the orchid."

Jack would say it was a capitalistic gesture. I know he would. But it was a kind of royal gesture, too, like a king would make. I couldn't straighten it out in my mind. A person had to have money to make a royal gesture, but if you had money, that made you a capitalist, and that wasn't good.

The more I see things happen, the harder it gets to figure out what the truth is. Maybe when I have my own beau who sends me things, instead of watching what happens when Beatrice's beaux send her things, it will be easier for me to pick out the truth. It's very complicated now. It's interesting, though.

Thirteen

☙ BEATRICE is a flirt. She never will marry Jake whatever his name is. I found that out when Beatrice took me to my first dance at Cornell. Father had come back from France and Mother went home with him, so Beatrice was stuck with me for the Easter vacation. Maybe it was because I was so bored at Westlake that I was really glad to see Beatrice when I got off the train at Aurora—that's where she was going to college.

Whatever the reason was, I was really glad to see Beatrice. And she acted glad to see me. She was nice to me, really nice. She teased me in front of her friends—she seemed to have a million friends—but it wasn't mean teasing. I was almost deciding to make her my best friend when we went to Cornell and I found out she was a flirt. She was just like Becky Sharp, that awful woman in *Vanity Fair.*

Right after I got off the train, she'd taken me to a place called The Idiot's Delight and bought me a Mount Everest. They are big high mountains of chocolate ice cream with marshmallow for snow and maraschino cherries for the mountain climbers. "I'm taking you to a dance at Cornell," she told me.

"A dance! I've never been to a dance."

"I know your life history. I know you haven't."

"But I won't know what to do—"

"You'll dance."

"But I don't know how to dance—with somebody else."

"I'll teach you—we've got three days. You can learn to be Irene Castle in three days."

My hands got prickly—me at a ball! I had an awful thought. "I haven't got a ballgown."

"Oh, yes, you have. Mother sent one—she had Miss Perkins make it up in a hurry. And it is a ballgown! Marie Antoinette wouldn't mind wearing it."

"Oh, Beatrice, is it pretty?"

Beatrice looked at me for a minute."It's unusual," she said.

"Unusual? When can I see it?"

"As soon as you finish your Mount Everest."

It was a ballgown. It was unusual, too. It was lavender brocade—"from a dress of Gammie's," Beatrice said. It did look like a Marie Antoinette dress. It had a full skirt and a small waist, but it wasn't cut down low in the front, like Marie Antoinette's. I put it on.

"I don't look like Marie Antoinette."

"We're in luck. Imagine if Marie Antoinette suddenly popped up at Cornell."

"Where's your dress?" I asked Beatrice.

"Mother sent me one—she wanted me to look like the real Beatrice."

"Who's that?"

"Who is that? Who is she, do you mean? Beatrice is the lady Dante wrote about."

"Let me see the dress," I said.

Beatrice pulled a long scarf from a box. "Is that a dress?" I asked. "It's nothing but a piece of goods."

"That's right," Beatrice said. She slipped it over her head. It turned into a dress of a million pleats. It was blue—blue-lavender—the colour of the gentians that grow up on the mountains in Colorado. It was the colour of Beatrice's eyes. It turned her into one of the goddesses in my mythology book. The huntress one. Without the bow and arrows.

"It's a dress from Florence," Beatrice said. "Mother saw it in *The New York Times*. It's a Fortuny, whatever that means."

"It's the most romantic dress I ever saw in my life," I said.

Beatrice pulled it over her head. "Now don't you start that," she said in a cross voice. "I wish you and Mother would stop being romantic all the time. I wish you'd climb out of the books you read and live like other people."

"Beatrice! You don't want to be like other people!"

"I do, too," said Beatrice. "I want to be exactly like other people. I wouldn't be caught dead in that dress. I'm going to borrow one of Virginia's. She's my roommate. You'll meet her in a minute. Come on, we better start dancing." She put a record on the Victrola. It was 'The Blue Danube.' "Now, Babe, this is a waltz. You make squares." She started counting, "One, two, three."

We danced for three days, between Mount Everests

at The Idiot's Delight. We danced on the platform while we waited for the train to Ithaca—where Cornell is. Virginia and the girls who lived in the next room, and four or five other girls, came down to see us off. When the train came in, they all waved and yelled, "Have a good time, Babe!" And, "Remember, Babe, one, two, three!" It was fun.

It got serious after the train started. Beatrice said, "Now we just have time for me to give you some pointers." Before I could open my mouth, she said, "Getting along with men isn't one bit like it is in books. The first thing to remember is to listen. Don't tell them what you think, don't tell them how you feel. For Pete's sake don't tell them your plan to have eight boys and live in a big house in the country—when you're not living in a hotel."

I didn't tell her I had a new idea since Jack sent me an article about environment versus heredity. I was going to have eight babies with fathers from eight different countries, take them to an island and see if environment or heredity won. "Oh, Beatrice, I haven't wanted to do that for years and years."

"Well, you've probably figured out something else to do that's just as crazy. Don't talk about it, whatever it is. Men don't like girls who think differently."

"Father likes Mother, and she thinks differently."

"That's different. Father is simple about Mother."

"Father is not simple!"

"All right. All right! Let's not get into a big fight now. There isn't time. Just listen to me. I know what I'm talking about."

I remembered Jake and the orchids. "Go on," I told her.

"Don't talk," Beatrice said. "Don't talk. Just listen. That's all there is to it."

"I know that," I said. "Mr. McClintock told me you'll never get in trouble if you keep your bowels open and your mouth shut."

"Oh, for heaven's sake, don't say that!" Beatrice screamed. "Just don't say anything. Just look as if everything they were saying was perfectly wonderful—even if you don't think it is."

"I wouldn't like a man I had to be a hypocrite with," I said.

"Look, Babe, you're not going to marry this man. You're just going to dance with him. Forget for one night that you are the great honest heroine, the partner who fights shoulder to shoulder with her I.W.W. husband—"

"Beatrice!"

"All right, I'm sorry, but you are so like Mother—"

"Me? Like Mother? You're crazy."

"Oh, yes you are. You are both playing parts from books or something all the time. This once, don't play any part. Don't do anything except make small talk."

"I don't know how to make small talk."

"Oh, Lord, we should have practised that in the last three days." Beatrice took hold of both my hands. "Peakie, please. Tonight may be the most important night of my life. Please. It's really important. I'll give you my Fortuny dress if—"

I pulled my hands away. I looked out of the window. "I

know what you want," I said at the window. "You want me to keep still. Don't worry. I won't say a word. Not One Single Word."

"Oh, dear, you—" Beatrice started when the conductor shouted, "Ithaca next stop." Then she got so busy looking at herself for the hundredth time in the mirror in her purse and putting powder on her nose from her Doreen, she forgot to finish.

I didn't look at myself, but I was excited. Not because I was going to see the man who was going to take me to the ball—Beatrice said I wouldn't meet him until later—but because I was going to see Jake. I hoped he'd like me, if he was going to be my brother-in-law. I was sure I'd like him. All those orchids—that was very royal. I liked that.

And when a very tall, thin man with a fur coat like the robe we use in the Ford on cold days yelled, "Heh, Beatrice!" I did like him. Right away.

After Beatrice ran to meet him and he gave her a big bear hug, she turned to me and said, "This is Hank. Hank, this is Babe."

I looked at her. "Where's Jake?"

Beatrice's mouth got so thin that you would have thought she didn't have any lips. The man who wasn't Jake stopped hugging Beatrice. "Who's Jake?" he said.

"Jake's the man who sent—" I started, but Beatrice interrupted me with, "Oh, the child is so excited about coming to Cornell, she doesn't know what she's saying."

Then she looked up at the man who wasn't Jake, who was Hank, and said, "Nobody else, absolutely nobody else in the world would be dear enough to invite my little sister, too. It was exciting enough to have the handsomest man on the campus ask me down, but to have him be the kindest one on the campus, too. It's really too divine!"

She said it in a fluttery voice I had never heard her use in her life before. Never. It was so disgusting I thought it would make Hank throw up. When I looked at him, he didn't look as if he was going to throw up. He was smirking. Smirking!

It was the last time I looked at him until we got into a taxicab—the three of us all squidged together into the back seat, with Hank in the middle. It was raining. When we went around corners, the streets were so slippery that the taxicab would skid, and if Hank fell against Beatrice he'd say, "Your corner."

And she'd laugh and say, "I'm so lucky!"

When he fell against me, he'd say, "Your corner." I didn't laugh. I didn't say a thing.

I didn't say a thing, either, when we got into the lobby of the hotel and Beatrice's suitcase opened up and her things spilled all over the carpet. I didn't help her pick them up. I didn't need to. Hank rushed to pick up some of the stuff, and other men came rushing up to pick up the rest of it. The lobby was crowded with men. I never saw so many men together outside of the Labour Temple.

After we got to our room, after the bellboy left—I wish bellboys wouldn't always open the door to the bathroom before they leave; it always embarrasses me—I said to Beatrice, "I want to say something to you."

Beatrice started to unpack. "I haven't time to listen."

"You'd better listen to me. If you don't listen, I'll say it right in front of that Hank."

"Oh, all right, but hurry up." She sat down on the edge of one of the beds.

"I just want to tell you, don't you ever talk about Mother and me acting again. You're worse than both of us."

Beatrice fluttered her eyelashes. That was silly of her to do to anybody in the family; we all knew it was a signal that she was going to tell a lie. "I haven't the vaguest idea what you're talking about," she said.

"I saw you fiddle with that lock thing on your suitcase. You made it open on purpose. I know you did."

"Now, Babe—"

"Don't call me Babe. And you did fiddle with it. I saw you."

"Peakie, dear, you don't understand—it was a swell way to meet a lot of men."

"What do you want a lot of men for? You've got that Hank."

"Oh, Babe—I'm not sure I've got him. I want to make him a little jealous."

"That is the cheapest thing I ever heard of in my entire life. At least if I pretend I'm somebody, I don't pretend to be a cheap flirt like Becky Sharp. I'm somebody good, like—like Edith Cavell, and I rescue English soldiers from the Germans."

Beatrice was getting mad. "All right, Miss Goody Two-Shoes! Just wait until you have a beau before you get so high and mighty, Miss Babe. And if you go around sulking, not saying a word, or blurting out the first thing that comes into your head, you never will have a beau." She got up. "Why, oh why did you have to say that about Jake?"

"I thought he was going to be here. You were engaged to him at Christmastime."

"I was not engaged to him. Not officially engaged. Then I met Hank after Christmas, and I knew he was the one."

"What happened to Jake? When you told him about Hank?"

"Oh, you are such a baby. I didn't tell him about Hank."

"What did you tell him?"

"I'm not going to tell you—you'll make a big speech about me being like Becky Sharp." She walked over and looked at herself in the long mirror that was on the back of the bathroom door. "Becky Sharp," she said to herself in the mirror. She pulled some of her hair so it made little curls in front of her ears. "Becky Sharp."

"Tell me," I said. "Tell me what you told him. I won't make any speeches. I promise."

"I'll tell you if you'll stop talking afterwards. We have to get started—we have to order a sandwich or something and take baths and—"

"I promise, I promise."

"Well, it was really very sad. He came up to Aurora, and we went for a walk in the snow, and I told him I couldn't marry him because—" She started to giggle.

"Why?" I asked. "Why couldn't you marry him?"

"Because he lived on a cattle ranch."

"What did that have to do with it?"

"That's what he said. I told him I couldn't marry him because"—she began to giggle again—"because the cows would give me hay fever."

"But that's not true. You've petted Priscilla millions of times when Father was trying to milk her."

"Of course it's not true. But I couldn't bear to hurt his feelings."

"I bet you hurt his feelings when you laughed."

"I didn't laugh when I told him, you ninny! I cried—a little. I let a tear come out of the corner of my eye, and I turned my head away to brush it off. He said I was very brave, not wanting him to see me cry."

"He never believed that."

"You don't know the first thing about men. Of course he believed it. He sent me a wire when he got back to Texas. It said he was trying to accept the cruel trick that fate had played on us as bravely as the bravest girl in the world had accepted it. That's me."

"If he believed you, why didn't he give up his cows? That's what the man I am going to marry would do. He would say all is well lost that's lost for love, like that poet said—I can't remember his name—"

"Well, you better plan to marry him when you remember it. No other man will give up what he likes or what he's used to for you. You'd better remember that if you want to get married. Men are just little boys—they want everything. The trick is to make them want you."

"I don't want to marry a little boy. I don't want to marry anybody if I have to play tricks to get him. I wouldn't play tricks on a friend."

"Men aren't friends, for heaven's sake—they're beaux."

"My beaux will be friends," I said.

"Well, then, make up your mind you're going to be an old maid."

"I don't want—"

"Or if you're lucky, you can marry an old fuddy-duddy like that professor in your precious *Little Women.*"

"I don't want to—"

"Stop it!" Beatrice shouted. "This isn't the time to discuss your future. Not if you want to go to the dance."

"The ball! The ball!" I shouted. "I'd forgotten all about the ball!"

"Well, hurry up or you'll miss it. And stop calling it a ball. It's a dance. It isn't a ball."

She was right; it wasn't a ball. It wasn't even a dance, or anyway it wasn't like any dance I had ever read about in any book or seen in any moving pictures. After we had taken a bath and eaten the sandwiches and put on our dresses, we went down to the lobby. Beatrice whispered to me as the elevator got to the first floor, "Remember, don't talk." She put on her fluttery look and got off the elevator.

Hank was there, waiting right by the elevator. Standing with him was a man with light hair. It was so light that it looked like white hair. He was short, a lot shorter than Hank. He had a pink and white face, a round face like the doll baby I had at home. If that is the man who is going to take me to the ball, I thought, I am going to die. I am going to fall right down here on this red carpet and die.

It was the man. Hank said his name was Claude—and we ought to like each other because "Claude lives in the country, too, on a farm," Hank said—and of course I didn't die. I guess if I died every time I wanted to, I'd have to have more lives than cats are supposed to have.

We all got into a taxicab. This time, Hank and Claude sat on those funny little seats that plump down, because, Hank said, "I want to sit here and drink in the beauty of you two nymphs," but he just looked at Beatrice.

She started her fluttering again, and she fiddled with the pink chiffon scarf she had over her head. "I'm afraid my hair's a perfect mess." She had spent about a hundred hours in the room fixing every curl around her face and brushing out some little ones on the back of her neck.

I said, " 'A sweet disorder in the dress Kindles in clothes a wantonness."

"Babe!" Beatrice said.

Hank let out a loud hoot. "Babe," he said, "you are quite a babe!"

Claude didn't say anything. He didn't say anything in the taxicab. He didn't say anything going up the stairs. He didn't say anything when we walked into a big square room where a band was sitting up on a platform. An ugly big square room. It looked like a room in the Labour Temple. It had red-and-white banners pinned on the wall and red-and-white streamers instead of American flags, but the chairs that were all around the wall were the same varnished wood chairs as the ones at the Labour Temple.

He didn't say anything after Beatrice and Hank went whirling off. He took my right hand and held it straight out, he put his other hand in the middle of my back, and he started to walk forward. I would have fallen backward if I hadn't grabbed hold of his collar. He stopped walking to straighten it up.

"I'm sorry," I said before I remembered I wasn't supposed to say anything. He started walking forward again. I started trying to walk backward. He just wanted to walk —it wasn't anything like dancing with Beatrice at Aurora; maybe he had never heard of the squares and the 1, 2, 3's. Maybe it was because I was taller than he was, so I bent over, and it wasn't quite so bad. Until I passed a mirror and saw myself. My behind was sticking way far out.

The sweat started to roll down my face. I looked down at him—there was sweat all over his face, too. I was just trying to figure out how I could get my handkerchief —it was down the front of my dress where Beatrice told me to put it and Claude's head was right there on top of it—when the music stopped. Claude took out his handkerchief and wiped his face. I felt around inside my dress, but I couldn't find mine. It had slipped down inside my combination. It fell out when I got undressed at the hotel.

Hank and Beatrice came up, still dancing though there wasn't any music. "Having fun?" Hank asked.

"Yes, thank you. Can I speak to you a minute?" I said to Beatrice.

"What is it?" she said. "You're not supposed to—" I dragged her away.

"He won't talk," I whispered. "He can't dance and he won't talk. I know—I'm not supposed to talk. But isn't he supposed to talk? Isn't he supposed to say something? He hasn't said a word, not one word."

She looked over at Claude. "He's probably the shy kind," she said. "You'll have to talk, I guess. It's risky, but—don't say anything."

"Don't say anything!"

Beatrice said, "I mean, don't tell him anything. Ask him questions."

"What kind of questions?"

Hank started to walk up to us. Beatrice said in a hurry, "Oh, you know—what does he do? What does he like to do? Things like that—" and she waltzed into Hank's arms and they danced off.

Claude stood there. "Let's talk," I said. "Let's sit down and talk." He nodded, so I walked through the dancers to the row of chairs and sat down. Claude came and sat down next to me. He didn't look at me. When I said, "What do you do?" he turned his head my way.

"Go to college," he said.

"Well, what do you want to do?" I said.

"Graduate."

Nobody said anything. Then I thought of another question. "Well, what do you want—" I was going to ask him what he wanted to be when he grew up, but I never got the chance to ask it because a man stopped in front of us and said, "Hi, Claude. Is this the girl?"

When Claude said, "Yes," the man said, "my name is Harvey. Can I have this dance?"

I said, "No, thank you, I have a partner." Harvey looked at Claude, gave a kind of shrug, and walked away.

I found out then that Claude could talk. Loud. "Listen," he yelled. "You always dance with anyone who asks you! That was a friend of mine. You were supposed to dance with him." He was so mad that his face wasn't pink and white any more. It was red.

"I want my sister," I said to him.

I must have looked funny, because his voice got quiet when he said, "I'll get her," and he came back in a second with Beatrice and Hank.

"I want to go home," I said to Beatrice. But it wasn't Beatrice who took me back to the hotel. Hank took me.

And Beatrice is absolutely wrong when she says men can't be friends, because when we got in the taxi I started to cry, and when Hank put his arm around me and I told him about how funny I looked in the mirror and how I wasn't supposed to talk and how loud Claude had yelled at me when I wouldn't dance with that Harvey, he told me that Claude was a hick and he was a boob, too, not to be nice to such a nice girl as I was and that he, Hank that is, was a boob himself to have picked such a boob to take me to my first dance even though he, Hank that is, didn't know it was my first dance and would I forgive him and be his friend? And I told him of course I would forgive him and be his friend, and he gave me his handkerchief and he bought me a Hershey bar when we got to the hotel, and he went up in the elevator with me and took the key and opened the door for me, and he asked me if I'd be all right, and after I had told him I'd be fine and after he said good night and started down the hall, he turned back and said, "You go on saying anything that comes into that nice head of yours. It won't keep you from going to lots of dances and having lots of beaux. You wait and see."

And he gave me a quick hug, and he ran down the hall to the elevator. I hope Beatrice marries Hank. That's very disloyal to Jake, but I never saw Jake, and I've seen Hank.

Fourteen

I THREW the Book into the Potomac. The Book with the things I wasn't going to do when I grew up in it. When I had my own children. The Book that Mother told me to start back in Marlborough a long time ago, before I went to school. To any kind of school. I threw it away because I was mad at Mother, and I threw it in the Potomac because I was in Washington and that's where the Potomac is.

I had started to write in it, "Don't decide things that will change your daughter's entire life without talking to her first." But I was so mad at Mother, so furious-mad at Mother, that I said out loud—and I was so mad that it didn't make any difference if somebody did walk by my room and hear me talking to myself—"I don't need any book to remember what to do or not to do! All I have to remember is what Mother does and do the opposite," and I threw the Book right out the window.

Then it suddenly hit me that it would be just like one of the ninnies here to pick it up and read it and think it was so funny that she'd read it to all the other ninnies. I bolted down the stairs. But nobody had picked it up before I got to the courtyard where it was lying on the grass, so I picked it up and walked out of Miss Lothrop's School, out onto the street, and I kept on walking until I came to the Potomac and I threw the Book in it.

That's where I was—I was at Miss Lothrop's School in Washington—and that's why I was so mad at Mother. She had decided to send me to Miss Lothrop's and she hadn't bothered to ask me if I wanted to go. I thought in the summertime it was kind of funny I wasn't being tutored up at Sakuragawa where I was at camp, because even though I had gone to all those classes after Christmas for the girls who had been sick, I knew I was still way behind the other girls in my class at Westlake.

But when I wrote to Mother and asked her if she hadn't better do something, write to my counsellor or something, she wrote back, "Don't worry—everything's going to be fine. Swim a little, hike a little. Get more freckles. Come home prepared for a great big glorious surprise!" And though I begged her once a week, in that letter you have to write home every Sunday at camp, to tell me what the surprise was, she wouldn't. And when I wrote Father, a special, private letter to the Store and begged him to tell me, he wrote back, "I can't, Peakie dear. It's a surprise." So I spent the summer trying to figure out what it was.

I had plenty of time to figure. The only time I went swimming was when I was dirty and wanted to get clean, and I had to feel very dirty to get into the water at Sakuragawa, because there were leeches in the water, black, slimy leeches—and they were flat. They get on your legs, and they won't get off without the most disgusting fight.

And after the first hike I told Miss Cross, the head counselor, that I wouldn't ever go on another hike again, and I didn't care if they sent me home because I wouldn't go. It was because of the counsellor in charge of hiking, Miss Abernathy. She wore men's shirts and men's pants that she had cut off so they stopped above her knees, and somebody should have told her she shouldn't have cut them off, because her legs were very fat above her knees and nobody would ever have known if she hadn't cut off the pants. Miss Abernathy, though she always shouted when I called her Miss Abernathy—"It's Bobby to my fellow campers, just Bobby, and you know it, you funny, funny girl. You're trying to get my goat, ha-ha." And she'd glare at me—Miss Bobby Abernathy told us the name of every tree we hiked by and every bush we hiked by, and if a bird happened to be on a tree or on a bush, she told us the name of the bird.

And after we had stopped hiking and had unwrapped our sleeping bags and made the fire and cooked the hot dogs, she asked us so many times if we didn't think the pine cones smelled great in a fire outdoors and if we didn't think the hot dogs tasted great when they were cooked outdoors and if we didn't think the Big Dipper looked great when you were lying on the ground outdoors that I decided I was never going to go hiking again.

They didn't send me home because I wouldn't go hiking, but I had to wait until I got home to find out what the surprise was.

Only I didn't go home. There wasn't any Marlborough any more. Not for us, anyway. Somebody had broken into it when Father was in France and Mother was at Shelton, and they'd taken all the things that Mother had marked Best—the Best Linens, the Best Blankets, the Best Silver. And Father said they must have known about furniture, even if it wasn't marked, because they had taken the Best Furniture.

It made Mother so sad she never wanted to see Marlborough again, so Father put an ad in the paper and somebody bought it. When I went back to Kansas City, I went back to the Missouri Manor. It was a hotel where Father and Mother were staying until they decided what to do.

It wasn't the kind of hotel with bellboys, where you come for one night and go away the next morning. It was the kind where you can stay for years and years if you want to. I don't know why anybody would want to. Nobody was there but grumpy old men who glared at you over the top of their newspapers when you forgot and ran through the lobby, and old ladies with grumpy old dogs who snarled at you when you tried to pat them. And married people who sat together at separate tables in the dining room, who'd talk to each other when they were deciding what to eat, who would say, "What vegetable are you going to have? Better take the string beans. The fresh peas are canned," and then they'd stop talking to each other.

None of the married people talked and laughed like Father and Mother, and Father and Mother didn't laugh as much as they used to after Mother told me about the surprise. Because when they did laugh, I sat there and glared at them until they'd stop laughing, and Mother would tell me to get up and leave the table.

I couldn't help glaring. Because the great big glorious surprise was Miss Lothrop's School. I wasn't going back to Westlake. I was going to Miss Lothrop's. Her school was in Washington. Aunt Hattie had gone to school in Washington when she was a girl, Mother told me, with her eyes opened very wide, the way they get when she's excited about something, and Aunt Hattie said they had been the most wonderful years of her life, and Father had asked Mr. McKee, who had a store in New York like Father's Store in Kansas City, which was the best school now in Washington, and Mr. McKee had said that the best one there now, without any question, was Miss Lothrop's—though I don't see why anybody should pay any attention to what a man in New York says about a school in Washington, certainly not a dumb man like Mr. McKee.

When Father told him that I didn't want to go to college after I finished school—I wanted to go to dramatic school—Mr. McKee said to Father, "A sound idea! It will give her poise so she won't be nervous when she's on committees in the Junior League and has to stand up and make a motion." The Junior League! Me in the Junior League! Jack would never speak to me again if I was in the Junior League. That showed how dumb Mr. McKee was.

When Mother told me about Miss Lothrop's, I said, "What's the matter with Westlake?"

Mother said, "You tell me! All you've ever told me about

Westlake was that you were bored to death there. You're the only child I ever knew who said she was bored. But you said it."

I wanted to tell her maybe I was the only child that ever said it out loud, but I bet I wasn't the only child that was ever bored. You're bored—for great hunks of time—when you're young. I bet she was bored for great hunks of time when she was young—why couldn't she remember? But I didn't. I didn't tell her. I didn't want to get into a big fight about being bored. I wanted to go back to Westlake.

"I wasn't crazy about it," I said. "But I figured out it was because I was sick, and it was a new place and I was a new girl and I didn't know anybody. This year I won't be a new girl and—"

"This year you're going to Miss Lothrop's," Mother said. "You're going to have to repeat a year anyway, so the girls you knew at Westlake will be a year ahead of you. At Miss Lothrop's you can start off with a clean slate. And you'll be in the most exciting city on the globe right now, where the League of Nations is being planned. It's going to change the entire world. And you'll be there while they're changing it. Think of that!"

"I want to go back to Westlake," I said.

"Peakie Maston," Mother said. "For once in your life—no, for once in my life, just once before I die—do you think you could arrange to surprise me? Do you think you could not argue about something I want you to do? Do you think that once, just once, you could just do it?"

"I still want to go back to Westlake," I said.

"Well, I can surprise you if you can't surprise me," Mother said. "I am through arguing. You are going to Miss Lothrop's. Go put that in your pipe and smoke it."

I was so mad at her that I never talked to her unless I had to the whole time before Father and I got on the Santa Fe to go to Miss Lothrop's. I knew I was rotten. I knew it was a rotten thing to do.

I wasn't only rotten to Mother. I was rotten to everybody. I was rotten to Aunt Hattie. When she came to see us and told me, "These are the happiest days of your life," then sighed and said, "I hope you realize youth is the happiest time of anybody's life," I ran out of the room. That was a rotten thing to do, but I was afraid if I stayed I'd tell her what I was thinking—that if youth is the happiest time of anybody's life, it must be a perfectly, terribly unhappy time when you grow up. If it is any worse than it is now, I don't see how grownups can stand it. Maybe they get used to it. Maybe they don't remember how unhappy it was when they were young.

I was even rotten to Benny. She called me up at the Missouri Manor and asked me to come and see her. The man at the desk called a taxicab for me, and it took me to the big house where Benny was working. There were three children, two boys and a girl, in the family she was with now, and they were waiting on the porch with Benny for me to come, and I was so jealous that they had Benny now for their friend and I didn't that I only stayed for a minute. I didn't even stay long enough to eat any of the marble cake with peppermint icing that Benny had made for me because she knew it was my favourite kind of cake. I never asked her about Willy.

I couldn't help it. I couldn't help being rotten. I tried thinking about what Father said, about how he felt every day was like a page in his autobiography. I tried thinking about the way I felt—that I was acting in a moving picture, and I knew I was acting so rotten that I wouldn't want my children to look at the part of the moving picture I was acting in then, but it didn't help.

I couldn't think about my children. I couldn't think about anything except that I was going to Washington. Going to a new school again, where I was going to be a new girl again. A new girl who was older than all the other girls in the class. And I was going back to the seat in the dark moving picture house. I was going to watch a movie that I wasn't going to be in. It was going to be a new movie, but I wasn't going to be in it. Again.

And then, as if it weren't bad enough, everybody started going topsy-turvy. Father was the first one. He laughed at me. Father has never laughed at me. Never. In all the almost fifteen years I've known him, he has never laughed at me. But on the Santa Fe, he laughed at me.

The porter had barely put the bags up on the rack and asked if we wanted a pillow and if we wanted to eat in the drawing room before Father said, "Peakie, I'm not at all proud of the way you've been acting since you came home. You've been making your mother very unhappy."

And I was so rotten that I told him what I had vowed I would never tell him in my whole life because I knew it would hurt his feelings. I said, "I don't want to hurt your feelings, but I don't like Mother. I wish I never had to see her again."

Father said, "You're not hurting my feelings. It would be your loss if you never saw your mother again—you'd miss seeing a genius."

"A genius! Mother's not a genius! She can't write or paint or any of those things."

"She can marry a young man, a very serious young man —so serious he thought, 'Life was real! Life was earnest! And the grave was not its goal.' He believed, really believed, he had to 'be up and doing, With a heart for any fate; Still achieving, still pursuing, Learn to labour and to wait.' And she married the serious young man and loved him. She loved him with so much joy, she made living such a joy, that she turned his life into a party. And he didn't have to wait for the party to begin. With your mother, it begins every morning and it keeps right on going. The party never stops. That takes genius." Father looked straight at me. "And your mother has it. I married a wife who is a genius!"

"Well, Father," I said, "your wife who is such a genius has just ruined my life."

And Father laughed! "My daughter's life is ruined! Ruined at fourteen!" He laughed so hard that he had to get out his handkerchief and wipe the tears out of his eyes.

"I'm almost fifteen. And Mother has ruined my life," I told him. "She's always ruined it."

"Oh, now, Peakie!" Father said. "Nobody ruins anybody else's life. They don't even have to try. People—

most people anyway—are very good at ruining their own lives. They don't need any help from anybody else."

"Mother has ruined my life."

"How did she go about it?" Father asked.

"Well, she laughs at me all the time, the way you're laughing at me now. She makes fun of me—she's always teasing me—"

"She teases you because she loves you and—"

"Because she loves me!" I interrupted.

"Have you ever seen her tease anybody she didn't like? And she's a woman with strong dislikes."

"No, I guess not," I said. "But she embarrasses me, too. We never go any place that people don't look at her—"

"Well, she's quite a sight. I don't blame them," Father said.

"I don't mean just look. They eavesdrop, too."

"Why of course they do!" Father said. "They don't get a chance to listen to a joyful woman every day of their lives."

"And she never calls me pet names, like lamb. She calls you lamb. Sometimes she even calls Beatrice lamb. She's never once called me lamb. Not once."

"Perhaps," said Father, "if you stopped being as bristly as a porcupine most of the time with her, if you gave up being a porcupine and acted like a lamb, she might call you a lamb."

I couldn't talk for a minute. "I still haven't told you the big thing."

"All right," Father said. "What's the big thing?"

"The big thing is that she's sending me to Miss Lothrop's—she's sending me to a new school. To a new school where I have to try to get acquainted all over again with new people and things. And she didn't even ask me if I wanted new people and things."

"She paid you a great compliment. She thinks you're strong enough and brave enough to face new people—and things. She's paid you an even bigger compliment—she thinks you've got enough imagination to enjoy it. I hope she's right." He looked at me and smiled, the first real Father one he'd smiled since we'd gotten on the Santa Fe. "I think she is," he said.

Fifteen

FATHER wasn't the only one who went topsy-turvy. Jack changed, too, or his letters changed, and they were the only way I could find out that he changed. I couldn't see him. I hadn't seen him since the morning he hugged me and said, "Don't forget."

He began to change after I had been to New York. I wrote to him everything about New York—everything I felt about New York. I had promised him at Marlborough I would write to him everything. He wasn't half as crazy about New York as I was. That was all right. He had London. But when I told him what had been worrying me ever since I'd seen New York, he changed from a friend into a teacher—a teacher who was disgusted with me.

I had told him the one thing about New York that worried me—I couldn't figure out how to live in Mark Twain's house without being a capitalist. I didn't want to do any of the evil things he told me capitalists did: I didn't want to take money from the poor. I wanted everybody, not just the poor, to have enough money to do what they wanted to do and live where they wanted to live and give their children what they wanted to have.

I wanted to live in Mark Twain's house on Fifth Avenue and have my children live in Mark Twain's house. It was an elegant house—we would have to be elegant when we lived there. That was all right because I wanted us to be elegant. Not fancy-pancy elegant, but elegant-elegant. Like my hat from Tappé's—Henriette was absolutely right. I loved my Tappé hat— I called it my "ça y est hat" —because it was the first thing I had ever worn that made me feel elegant.

And I wanted to make royal gestures, like sending people coffins of orchids. I wouldn't send orchids, of course. Only men sent orchids, but I'd give a friend something he wanted more than anything in the world. Like a ship to Jack, because he had told me three times that he got fed up always having to go to the places where the captain of his ship wanted to go—that Jack would like to go to the places where he wanted to go. That was his idea of the freedom of the seas.

I wrote him I was worried because I wanted to be elegant, but I didn't want to take money away from poor people—from any people. I wrote him, "Maybe I'm a pig, and I promised David Hayes I wouldn't be a pig. Maybe I'll have to choose the way David said. But can't you help me figure out how I can be elegant and not take money away from people?"

And he called me a silly girl. He called me a silly girl, and he said my letter was the silliest letter he had ever read from anybody. He said there was no point bothering him with such a silly question. Because it wouldn't make any difference what answer he gave to me. It was already determined what I was going to do. The way I was going to think, even the way I was going to feel—they were already determined by how much money my father made. "Economic determination," he called it, and he said it had already spoiled my chances to be free—to have a chance to choose. He said he would send me some books on economics, but it was probably too late. I was already spoiled by Mammon.

His letter came three weeks after I'd come to Miss Lothrop's. It scared me—it was so like those stories where the heroine is in some terrible trouble and she escapes and rushes through the dark to a house and knocks on the door and stands panting and saying to herself, "Now I'm safe," and the door opens and her terrible trouble is standing there. Jack's going topsy-turvy wasn't my terrible trouble, but it was scary.

Beatrice went topsy-turvy, too. That was lovely, a lovely surprise. It wouldn't have been such a surprise if I hadn't been too rotten at the Missouri Manor to notice anything. For the week she was there, Beatrice asked me into her room every night while she was getting dressed to go out with her beau. She had a new one—his name was Randy—and she'd tell me about him. "He's cute, Babe. And he dances like Joseph Santley. But sometimes I think if he says, 'You'd be surprised!' one more time, I'll step on his foot. No I won't. I'll jump down hard on both his feet," she told me while I powdered her back and helped her find her gloves.

The night Jack's letter got to Washington, it scared me so, I went straight to the telephone and called Beatrice. I called her collect. The minute I heard her voice, I burst into tears, which was funny—I hadn't cried during the whole time I was rotten.

"What's the matter, Babe? What's happened?" Beatrice said.

"Everything's awful," I told her. "Everything!"

"Well, anything special, honey?" Beatrice asked. Susan Perry told me in the infirmary that calling anybody "honey" was very common. I didn't care if she thought it was common or not—it sounded lovely when Beatrice said it.

"Miss Lothrop's School is awful," I said. "Miss Lothrop is awful. She's as cold as Mère Bernadette, but Miss Lothrop wears ground-gripper shoes when she has on her black chiffon evening dress. And a silver Indian necklace she got in Taos. She's crazy about Indians. They're so simple, she says."

"Oh, for heaven's sake!" Beatrice said. "She sounds awful. What else is awful?"

"Father laughed at me on the Santa Fe. And Jack thinks I'm spoiled by Mammon and—"

"Spoiled by who?" Beatrice interrupted.

"By Mammon. And he says it's too late to do anything about it, and I don't think he wants to be my friend any more—" I started to cry so hard that I couldn't talk.

"Honey," Beatrice said. "Honey, listen to me. It's your sister talking—your awful sister. It's growing up that's awful—that's all it is. Honestly, I know. Its just growing up that's awful."

"Well, being grown up will be just as awful," I sobbed.

"That's not so," Beatrice said. "To quote an old Chinese philosopher, 'You'd be surprised!' "

I almost laughed. I knew the old Chinese philosopher was really that Randy, but then I started to cry again because he made me think of the Missouri Manor and those married couples who sat there and never said a word to each other after they'd decided what vegetable they were going to have.

"I've seen lots of grown-up people, Beatrice, and they look awful. They look miserable!"

"Oh, they're the boobs," Beatrice said. "Honey, they're just the poor boobs—they don't know how to have fun. You're not a boob. You're going to have a fine time."

"When?" I asked her. "When? When is it going to start?"

"Sooner than you think. It will start—you won't even know it's starting. You'll just wake up some day and you'll say, 'Why, I'm having a fine time.' Honest, Babe. That's the way it will happen."

"But when will it happen?" I sobbed at her. "When will the fine time begin?"

"Oh, Babe, I can't tell you that," Beatrice said. "But it won't be long. In a year or two you'll—"

"A year or two!"

"Maybe sooner. Just hold on. It will come. I promise you, Babe. The fine time will come."

The fine time came, and it came sooner than a year, sooner than a year or two. It came exactly three weeks and four days and eighteen hours after Beatrice had promised me it would. It came at three o'clock in the afternoon on Saturday, the fourth of November, one week before Armistice Day.

It started when I said, "You could strike if you were organized," and Lacy said, "Well, come on. Let's get organized."

I hadn't paid any attention to Lacy—to Lacy Ames. I'd noticed her face because she looked healthy—she had tan left over from summer, or maybe in California where she comes from the tan never does leave—and she had pink cheeks, but she looked pretty, too, and it's unusual to see somebody who looks healthy and pretty, too. They usually look too healthy to look pretty. But I'd never spoken to her until the Saturday before Armistice Day.

Everybody was out in the courtyard. Nobody was doing anything special—it was warm even though it was November—and nobody was talking about anything special until a girl came charging through the gate, yelling, "It's a disgrace! It's a disgrace!"

Then a lot of girls ran up around her and said, "What is it, Ruth? What's a disgrace?"

"Every other school in Washington," Ruth announced in a loud voice, "every single other school in Washington, D.C., is going to have a free day on Armistice Day except"—she paused for a big dramatic moment—"except guess which school?"

"Miss Lothrop's," somebody guessed.

"Miss Lothrop's is the correct answer," Ruth said, and everybody groaned.

They groaned loud at first, then they groaned soft, but they kept on groaning until it made me sick, really sick. I shouted at them, "Stop it! Stop all that silly moaning! If you want a free day so much, do something about it. But Stop Moaning!"

They stopped! They stopped, and all of them looked at me. Lacy walked up to me. "What can we do?" she asked.

"You could strike," I said, "if you were organized."

"Well, come on," Lacy said. "Let's get organized."

I didn't answer her. I walked across the court and through the gate to the street. And that was the minute, the exact minute, that the fine time began, because Lacy came running after me.

"Why did you go?" she asked. "That's a wonderful idea!"

"It's a silly idea," I said, and kept on walking.

"It's not a silly idea," Lacy said. She shuffled her feet to get in step with me. "You mean, nobody go to class on Armistice Day?"

"That's what a strike is. Nobody goes to work."

"Do you know how they get strikes started?" Lacy asked.

"Yes, I know all about them," I said. "Mother and I learned at the Labour Temple."

"Well, then, why did you walk out? Why didn't you stay and explain how they work?"

"Those girls wouldn't listen to me."

"They listened when you told them to stop moaning." Lacy laughed. "They probably were too shocked to moan. It was the first time they'd ever heard you talk."

"I can talk."

"They know that now." Lacy laughed. She stopped when she looked at me. "Oh, crackers, they knew it anyway. But everybody's been afraid to talk to you—"

"Afraid? Afraid of me? You're trying to get my goat."

"No, I'm not. Everyone's figured out you're the great brain—that you're so smart—"

"You *are* trying to get my goat!"

"No, honestly. You've always got a book in your hand —that's what's kept me from talking to you. I wouldn't open a book unless it's that or the dungeon."

"I carry a book around so I have something to do," I said. I looked straight at her. "So I'll have something to do if nobody talks to me."

"You see?" Lacy laughed. I had never seen a girl who laughed all the time the way Lacy laughed. "You see? That's a very smart thing to do, so you are smart."

"I'm not smart in school. I'm so dumb I don't know— I can't even remember what eight times seven is."

"Eight times seven? Crackers! You are dumb! That's simple. Eight times seven is—is—I haven't the faintest idea what eight times seven is."

"We're both dumb," I said.

Lacy said, "You're not dumb about strikes. How would you work it at Miss Lothrop's?"

"Easy," I said. "Nobody would go to classes."

"But Miss Lothrop would expel us, wouldn't she? Not

that I'd shatter into a million pieces if she did," Lacy said.

"She can't expel the whole school."

"That's right!" Lacy yelled. We were walking by the White House. The tourists turned away from the fence to look at Lacy. "What do you mean you're not smart? You're brilliant!"

"There's a problem, though," I said.

"What problem? Can I help? I'd love to help."

"We'll have to write a petition—we have to state the reasons why we are going to strike. And everybody's got to sign it. Everybody! If everybody doesn't sign it, it won't work. It would be wonderful if you'd help get people to sign. We've only got one week to get everybody's name on the petition—absolutely everybody's!"

Lacy and I walked on down Pennsylvania Avenue, planning our strike and kicking the leaves that were blowing along the sidewalk. We turned into a side street. Lacy was looking for a tearoom she said had heavenly chocolate mocha cake. When she saw a big pile of leaves by the curb, she put her hands up over her head, yelled, "Watch out below!" and dived into the pile. She came up with leaves stuck all over her sweater. They were stuck in her hair, too.

"Watch out below!" I yelled, and I jumped in with her.

Lacy pinched me. "Crackers! A policeman!" My head almost bumped into his knees.

"Here now, just what do you girls think you're doing?" the policeman said. "You ought to be ashamed of yourselves. I'll want your names, please."

I got up out of the leaves. I brushed them off my face.

I patted down my hair. I looked up at the policeman. "Please, officer," I said. I fluttered my eyelashes. "It wouldn't be Officer Ryan, would it?"

"No, it would not be Officer Ryan," he said.

"Would it be Officer O'Reilly?" Lacy asked.

"Never O'Reilly!" He smiled. "It's Bannon. It's Bannon, and you haven't answered my question yet, neither one of you. What do you girls think you're doing—messing up the street like that?"

Lacy climbed up out of the leaves. "We're organizing a strike."

Officer Bannon frowned at her. "A strike! What kind of talk is that for nice young ladies!"

I shook my head at Lacy. "She's got the word wrong, Officer Bannon. She hasn't any Irish in her, like you and me. It's not a strike we're planning." I grabbed Lacy's hand. "It's an uprising!"

We started running up the street. I turned around to shout at Officer Bannon, "Erin go bragh!"

He yanked off his helmet and waved it in the air. "Up the rebels!" he shouted back.

Lacy and I ran very fast up Pennsylvania Avenue to begin our strike, as fast as you can run while you're turning around to shout, "Up the rebels!" to a policeman and holding onto your friend's sweater because you're wobbly from laughing.